Jenny Quire

Omega Blessings!

Mike Rose

UNTANGLED

GOD'S GOOD NEWS
MAY BE BETTER THAN YOU THINK

MIKE ROSE

Published by Tetelestai Ministries, Portland

Editor: Pauline Wick
Book design: Rachel Plyler
Cover design: 99Designs
ISBN: 9798885676298

First Edition: November 2022
10 9 8 7 6 5 4 3 2 1

CONTENTS

INTRODUCTION

Perhaps the title of this book, *Untangled*, has stirred your curiosity. In most situations, tangles are bothersome at best. In others, they can be downright dangerous!

Our Granddaughters, Macy and Peyton, have beautiful long hair. I have witnessed many tears over the years as my wife, Deenie (aka "Mamie"), has combed out the painful tangles.

In our Southeast Alaska waters, hungry and curious whales occasionally find themselves tangled in commercial fishing nets. Some entangled whales are set free by people specially trained to deliver them while other whales will swim throughout the rest of their lives tangled and encumbered. Not long ago, a humpback whale made it all the way from Southeast Alaska to Hawaii dragging a large commercial fishing net buoy!

Unfortunately, in this same way, many Christians are living their lives unknowingly entangled and burdened. The weight of religion, tradition, and inaccurate Bible teachings have caused many believers to experience lives of frustration where they should be experiencing lives of freedom!

Perhaps you've heard the saying, "You don't know what you don't know." Many of the teachings I will share in the following pages are lessons from my own journey of becoming untangled that I wish I would have learned forty-five years ago.

Through this book, I pray the Holy Spirit will free you from the tangles of accusation and condemnation and usher you into the fullness of life that Christ paid for you to experience! I pray that the Spirit of wisdom and revelation will fill you and bless you with valuable insights for living your life in joyful alignment with God's will for you.

Deenie and I have pastored the Juneau Christian Center in Juneau, Alaska for thirty-five years. We have two sons with families of their own: Benjamin and Heather and Justin and Whitney. They have blessed us with five grandchildren.

ONE

TWO TREES

"The devil did not tempt Adam and Eve to steal, to lie, to kill or to commit adultery; he tempted them to live independent of God." - Bob Jones, Sr.

It seems appropriate for us to start at the beginning with Adam and Eve and two trees.

The Lord God planted a garden eastward in Eden and there, he put the man he had formed.

"And out of the ground the Lord God made every tree grow that is pleasant to the sight and good for food. The tree of life was also in the midst of the garden, and the tree of the knowledge of good and evil."
Genesis 2:8-9 New King James Version (NKJV)

Very early in the existence of Adam and Eve, they became familiar with two trees in the garden. The Lord God created every tree in the garden and they were all pleasant to the sight and good for food. Still, scripture directs us to focus on the two trees in the center of the garden. Often, when scripture calls special attention to something in a verse, it's because there is a deeper meaning to explore.

When we consider the tree of life, we might certainly think of Jesus, who is called "the prince of life" (Acts 3:15). Jesus said of himself, "I am the resurrection and the life" (John 11:25) and later, "I'm the way the truth, and the life" (John 14:6). John also wrote of Jesus that "in Him was life and the life was the light of the world" (John 1:4). I'm not going out on a limb here to say that the tree of life represents Jesus.

Let's consider the other tree in the center of the garden: the tree of the knowledge of good and evil. While the name of this tree sounds good and noble, it's obviously not a good tree. Before Eve was created, God commanded Adam not to eat from that tree.

> And the Lord God commanded the man, saying, "Of every tree of the garden you may freely eat; but of the tree of the knowledge of good and evil you shall not eat, for in the day that you eat of it you shall surely die."
> Genesis 2:16-17

Why would God put the tree with poisonous fruit smack dab in the middle of the garden without childproofing it? It's obvious that our freedom of choice is important to our Heavenly Father. Without the freedom to reject him, we are powerless to choose him. Our obedience is a choice.

POISON IS NO PICNIC

Eating poisoned food is no picnic, I have firsthand experience. Early on in our marriage, my young bride, Deenie, fixed a large portion of delicious lasagna. It was in a big aluminum container and each time we wanted leftovers, she would reheat all the lasagna in that big aluminum pan.

One night, Deenie drove with a friend to another city to eat out, and before she left, she reheated the lasagna for me. It was the fourth time it had been reheated. The lasagna looked good and tasted good, but an hour later, I was not feeling good. I came home from unloading a truck and soon became violently ill. I will not discuss the nauseating details, but I called the elders of the church because I thought I was dying. They came, they prayed, and I lived.

Deenie and I didn't know that reheating the food in that aluminum pan multiple times would make the food toxic and dangerous to eat. There is no way I would have eaten that food had I known it would poison me.

Why would Adam and Eve eat something after they were warned by God that it would kill them?

THE TEMPTATION

Now the serpent was more cunning than any beast of the field which the Lord God had made. And he said to the woman, "Has God indeed said, 'You shall not eat of every tree of the garden?'"
Genesis 3:1

After creation is recorded in Genesis, the author refers to God as "the Lord God." The purpose for the addition of the word "Lord" is to keep man aware of the need to honor God's position of Lordship over them.

By contrast, in this significant exchange, Eve and the serpent simply refer to him as "God."

And the woman said to the serpent, "We may eat the

fruit of the trees of the garden; but of the fruit of the tree which is in the midst of the garden, God has said, 'You shall not eat it, nor shall you touch it, lest you die.'"
Genesis 3:2-3

Then the serpent said to the woman, "You will not surely die. For God knows that in the day you eat of it your eyes will be opened, and you will be like God, knowing good and evil."
Genesis 3:4-5

Eve knew what God had said regarding the tree. The devil's line of reasoning implies that God was not telling them the truth and that he was holding out on them.

Eve was being tempted to become more like God. What Eve seems to have forgotten was that she had already been made in God's image (Genesis 1:27)! The serpent's insipid lie was that there was something that she could do to become more like God.

Why did she think that she needed more? That she needed to be more? Why didn't she think she was enough?

We know she hadn't been comparing herself with other women. It's possible that Eve was drawn to the wisdom of the serpent. Perhaps he had been planting subtle seeds of discontent in her heart through conversations with him that prepared her for the full-blown lie of the devil.

Deceptions often come by degrees. Little by little, we can drift off course without knowing it. Sow a thought, reap an action; sow an action, reap a habit; sow a habit, read a character; sow a character, reap a destiny; sow a destiny, reap an eternity. It all starts with one thought.

What is it that causes people to long for what someone else has? Eve was in a beautiful paradise that was perfect in every way. She had the privilege to walk, talk, and commune with her creator, the Lord God.

TWO WAYS OF LIVING

Part of the tree's name and description is "the knowledge of good…". That doesn't sound bad. This tree could have just as easily been called "the rules tree;" "the self improvement tree;" or "the try harder tree."

The tree of the knowledge of good and evil is a biblical model or type of the law. The Apostle Paul said, the power of sin is the law (1 Corinthians 15:56). The Apostle Paul also identified the law as the ministry of death and the ministry of condemnation (2 Corinthians 3:7, 9).

These two trees represent two ways of life that we all get to choose between. The tree of the knowledge of good and evil distracts us from the source of life, who is Jesus. The tree of the knowledge of good and evil could be called "the trying tree," while the tree of life might be called "the trusting tree."

The law is like a mirror that can identify our blemishes but has no power to correct or help us. In fact, the law is regularly used to point out our sins, our faults, and our shortcomings. While the law was good, it wasn't good for us.

THE FALLEN NATURE

Our early parents, Adam and Eve, experienced firsthand the disastrous collateral damage of spiritual death and separation from trusting in the wrong tree. They committed high treason against God by trusting the wisdom of the serpent. They chose the tree that leads to death over the tree that leads to life.

After Adam and Eve ate the poisonous fruit, their first response was self inspection. Before eating, they had not even noticed their nakedness. They were covered with God's glory and their attention was on the Lord and the purposes he had created them for.

When they were confronted by God, they discovered something

new in their fallen nature as God called them to account for their actions.

> "...Have you eaten from the tree of which I commanded you that you should not eat?" Then the man said, "The woman whom You gave to be with me, she gave me of the tree, and I ate."
> Genesis 3:11b-12

Adam, when questioned by God, found the ability to masterfully blame both the woman and God: "It was the woman whom you gave to be with me." In turn, the woman blamed the serpent. This is when the blame game began and it's still negatively impacting marital harmony to this day.

A husband and wife were driving down a country road. The atmosphere in the car was silent and intense after an earlier argument they'd had. While passing a barnyard filled with pigs, goats, and mules, the husband saw an opportunity for a cheap shot and said, "Relatives of yours?"

"Yes," replied the wife. "Those are my in-laws."

THE TRIUMPH OF THE GIFT

Adam and Eve caved to the temptation. They died that day, just as God had warned. No, they didn't die physically, but their spirits died, producing separation and great loss within their relationship with God.

After their treasonous actions, they heard the Lord God as he walked in the garden in the cool of the day and they hid from him among the trees of the garden. It's sad that the trees created for their pleasure to eat from and enjoy had now become a place to hide from God.

The Lord called to Adam, "Where are you?" God obviously knew

Adam's geographical location. He was speaking to the state of their spiritual death. There's no way to fully describe the horrible collateral damage that ravaged humanity from that one decision to disobey and reject God's command.

The haunting question, "Where are you?" is for all of humanity living outside the life of God.

The wonderful news is that our God is loving, merciful, kind, and compassionate. In fact, in the very place God could have delivered immediate judgment upon man's first rebellious transgression, he instead prophetically promised grace through the work of their coming Savior:

> ...the Lord God said to the serpent: "Because you have done this, You are cursed more than all cattle, and more than every beast of the field; on your belly you shall go, and you shall eat dust all the days of your life. And I will put enmity between you and the woman, and between your seed and her Seed; He shall bruise your head, And you shall bruise His heel."
> Genesis 3:14-15

God prophesied to the devil that his head would be bruised by the woman's seed, which refers to Christ. The word "bruise" here is better translated in the Hebrew: to (mortally wound or crush) Satan's head.

The crushing of Satan's head happened on the cross. In the Bible, the word "head" symbolizes the seat of power for a nation or leader, so, when God speaks of crushing Satan's head, it refers to Jesus Christ destroying and dismantling Satan's power over this world.

Jesus said:

> "Now is the judgment of this world; now the ruler of this world will be cast out. And I, if I am lifted up from the earth, will draw all peoples to Myself." John 12:31-32

The place of the cross was on Golgotha. The word "Golgotha" means skull hill. Thus, as Christ is lifted up on the cross, his heel symbolically rested on the head of Satan himself. On that day, Jesus, the skull-crushing seed of Eve, was triumphant over the devil and his demonic hordes. He took back what had been stolen from Adam and rose victorious over all the works of darkness once and for all!

Once Christ claimed the victory over Satan, Father God made you and me alive with Christ, forgiving all our sins. He canceled our record of wrong, nailing it to the cross (Colossians 2:13-14).

> ...For this purpose the Son of God was manifested, that
> He might destroy the works of the devil.
> 1 John 3:8

The Greek word used here for "destroy" means: (to break up, destroy, and dissolve) the works of the devil.

> Therefore, as through one man's offense judgment came
> to all men, resulting in condemnation, even so through
> one Man's righteous act the free gift came to all men,
> resulting in justification of life.
> Romans 5:17-18

Through Jesus' finished work on the cross, the free gift of forgiveness, righteousness, and eternal life now belongs to us!

Through Christ, we can experience:

- LIFE OVER LAW
- RELATIONSHIP OVER RELIGION
- FAITH OVER FEAR
- JUSTIFICATION OVER CONDEMNATION
- MERCY OVER JUDGMENT
- GRACE OVER WORKS
- HEAVEN OVER HELL

While the future of our early parents looked dismal and hopeless, the God of all hope chose redemption over rejection.

It's so comforting to know that our loving Heavenly Father is omniscient, knowing everything from beginning to end. He's never surprised, confused, or shocked by turmoil in our lives. He specializes in damage control, transforming events that manifest as unmitigated disasters and turning them into something gloriously beautiful. He gives beauty for ashes, the oil of joy for mourning, and a garment of praise for the spirit of heaviness. Because of his loving eternal vantage point, we are able to trust him with all our hearts.

TWO

ABRAHAMIC COVENANT

"Any revelation from God's Word that does not lead us to an encounter with God only serves to make us more religious." - Bill Johnson

We were eight hours out of Anacortes, Washington on Eight Stars, a 42-foot Nordic Tug pleasure cruiser, on her maiden voyage. We were motoring through placid waters at ten knots and moving up the inside passage toward our destination of Juneau, Alaska. We were still 1,100 miles away and I found myself at the helm as the elderly owner, Kent, prepared to take a nap in the stateroom.

Before Kent went down for his nap, he gave me some quick instructions regarding the chart and compass and gave me a heading to follow. Though I was new to marine navigation, I felt confident that I could keep us on course. It was a perfect bluebird day, the water was calm, and I was enjoying the warm sunshine and beautiful scenery.

Three hours passed before Kent came up behind me and calmly said, "Pastor, we're being followed by a large U.S. Navy ship with its lights on."

"Good joke, Kent," I casually responded.

"No, really!"

Just then, I looked back and saw a large ship with lights on, and now, I also heard a siren blaring.

Kent quickly got on the radio with them and the naval officer said, "You are in a torpedo testing zone. Exit immediately!"

We complied and got out of the WG Active area torpedo test range near Nanoose Bay, British Columbia. So much for my first shift at the wheel.

I had the best intentions of being safe and staying on course. As a matter of fact, I thought I was on course! Ultimately, our wakeup call came in the form of a U.S. Navy ship.

This could have made for some interesting headlines: "Alaska-bound Nordic Tug Cruiser Torpedoed by Navy Submarine."

Being one degree off the proper setting, over a period of time, has the potential to take us into a perilous situation.

I am writing this book because I believe that there is a wakeup call for us as believers. I'm convinced that there is a doctrinal course correction for us to heed. We have already taken major hits from being a few degrees off in some of our established teachings.

COVENANT KNOWLEDGE

Covenants were very important in biblical history. In contrast, we in the Western world are much more familiar with contracts.

There are significant differences between covenants and contracts. Covenants carry a much greater level of commitment than a contract. A contract is usually a fifty-fifty proposition that specifies that I will do my part and I can expect that you will do your part. If either one fails to do their part, the contract is broken and becomes null and void. In order to sustain the contract, both parties must keep their end of the agreement.

Under a covenant, two people make an agreement with a commitment to one another that each one will do their part, no matter what the other person does.

Marriage is a covenant, not a contract. Have you noticed that vows are not: "I will give fifty percent to you, if you give fifty percent to me."

The wedding vows are covenant vows which are unconditional: "....for better, for worse; for richer, for poorer...."

A verse that shines the light of revelation for our understanding is in the book of Timothy:

> Be diligent to present yourself approved to God, a worker who does not need to be ashamed, rightly dividing the word of truth.
> 2 Timothy 2:15

Let's take a closer look and examine how we are to rightly divide the word of truth. Rightly dividing comes from the Greek word "orthotomounta" which means to cut straight. When we look at the Old Testament word for covenant, "Bereeth," we see that it means: In the sense of cutting —-a compact made by passing between pieces of flesh.

While this doesn't make the greatest sense to the Western mind, Timothy would have understood that "cutting straight" was a reference to covenant. In the East, they used the phrase, "to cut covenant." This phrase was also used for circumcision, which was the sign of covenant for the Hebrew male.

Could it be that we have drifted in our teachings because we missed a clue of monumental importance? I believe there has been a serious lack of understanding regarding the importance of covenants in the Bible.

Over the next two chapters, we are going to look at three main covenants God made with man throughout the Bible: the Abrahamic Covenant; the Mosaic Law Covenant; and, the New Covenant.

Chad Mansbridge in his book, *He Qualifies You* brilliantly defines each of the three major covenants with their distinct attributes and purpose. Clearly defining these covenants is key to more accurately understanding and interpreting scripture.

Under the Abrahamic Covenant, God's promises become your right and inheritance because of your pedigree (descendants).

Under the Mosaic Law Covenant, God's promises are your right and inheritance because of your performance.

Under the New Covenant, through the gospel of Jesus, God's promised blessings are your right and inheritance because of your position in Christ.

ABRAHAMIC COVENANT

The first covenant we will focus on is the Abrahamic Covenant recorded in the book of Genesis:

> Now the Lord had said to Abram: "Get out of your country, from your family And from your father's house, to a land that I will show you. I will make you a great nation; I will bless you and make your name great; and you shall be a blessing. I will bless those who bless you, and I will curse him who curses you; and in you all the families of the earth shall be blessed."
> Genesis 12:1-3

It's important to note that this Abrahamic covenant is full of grace for Abram (whom God later renamed Abraham) and his descendants. God said he would bless those who bless Abram and his descendants, and curse those who curse him. This covenant guaranteed to Abram and his descendants God's presence, his blessing, and his provision. There is no mention of judgment or correction for their bad behavior.

Abram went on to tell lies about his wife, Sarah, on two separate occasions, saying that she was his sister. He also allowed her to go into the harems of two heathen kings. Abram showed a lack of integrity and made poor decisions. Still, God continued to be faithful to his covenant promises. (Genesis 12:10-20)

Abram's descendants went on to make poor choices, as well. Here are a number of examples:

Abram's son, Issac, followed his father's example of lying and claiming that his wife was his sister. (Genesis 26:1-16)

Isaac's son, Jacob, manipulated his brother, Esau, to trade his birthright for a bowl of beans. With the help of his mother, Jacob deceived Isaac into giving him Esau's birthright blessing. God honored the blessing even though Jacob lied to get it. (Genesis 25:19-34; 27:1-41)

Jacob's sons, Simeon and Levi, deceived an entire town, murdering its men and plundering the town's possessions. (Genesis 34)

Reuben, Jacob's oldest son, had illegitimate sex with one of his stepmothers. (Genesis 35:22)

Judah, another son of Jacob, thought he hired a shrine prostitute for personal pleasure, only to discover that he had impregnated his daughter-in-law who had disguised herself as a prostitute. (Genesis 38:11-26)

Just when it seemed like Jacob's sons couldn't get any worse, they plotted their brother, Joseph's death and ended up selling him to slave traders, covering their tracks with lies and false evidence. (Genesis 37:12-36)

What's amazing is, despite all of this deplorable behavior, God does not rebuke or judge them. Instead, God continues to be faithful to his covenant with Abram by blessing his descendants.

When the Israelites left Egypt, God continued to treat them with grace despite their bad behavior. God delivered them from slavery and rescued them from Pharaoh's Army. When they complained to Moses that they were thirsty because the water tasted bitter, God worked a miracle by making the water sweet for them. (Exodus 15:22-16:35)

Later, when they wandered to Rephidim and discovered there was no water to drink, they complained and threatened to kill Moses. God, being gracious, provided water out of a rock. (Exodus 17:1-7)

Up to this point, God kept his covenant with Abram descendants by virtue of their birthright, not their behavior; their pedigree, not their performance. However, the wonderful grace covenant they were under was about to change.

THREE

THE COVENANT OF LAW

"All other religions are governed by a system of moral codes, rules, and laws. Christianity, on the other hand, is not a religion. It is a relationship. It is about having a relationship with Almighty God." - Joseph Prince

The law was a covenant that God made with the nation of Israel. It was his agreement with the Jewish nation. Leviticus 26:46 tells us:

These are the statutes, the ordinances and the laws that the Lord gave between Himself and the Children of Israel on Mount Sinai by the hand of Moses.

The Abrahamic Covenant was based on pedigree, which refers to the ancestry or descendants of Abraham.

At Mount Sinai, God introduced a law-keeping covenant to Moses that would radically transform the way God and his people would relate to one another. They were promised blessing if they obeyed, and cursing if they disobeyed.

Receiving God's blessing would require strict obedience to a lengthy list of commandments. A standard of performance was introduced as a means of earning God's blessing, and failure to meet these standards would result in judgment and a curse.

The people agreed to the Law Covenant, and Moses went back up the mountain for forty days. There, he received two stone tablets of the law, written with the finger of God. (Exodus 19:3-17)

While Moses was on the mountain receiving the Ten Commandments, the people were already breaking God's Law by worshiping a golden calf at the base of the mountain.

Moses came down from the mountain and said who is on the Lord's side and the tribe of Levi stepped up to administer judgment with the sword to those involved in pagan revelry and debauchery.

God's anger burned against his people because of their idolatry. For the first time in their history, God's anger was aimed at his covenant people and 3,000 were put to death.

Within three days under the Law Covenant, the people started complaining about their adversity. Complaining was nothing unusual under the Abrahamic Covenant because there had never been costly consequences. Now, post Mount Sinai, things were different. God sent fire from heaven and killed a number of them for complaining. (Numbers 11)

Soon after this, Miriam, the sister of Moses, murmured against Moses and was cursed with leprosy. (Numbers 12)

It wasn't too long after this that Moses sent twelve spies into Canaan to scout out the land. Two spies, Joshua and Caleb, were full of faith and brought back a positive report. The other ten spies gave a bad report, instilling fear in the hearts of the people. As a result, the ten spies died of a plague before the Lord.

There are many other examples of swift judgment coming upon God's covenant people after receiving this Law Covenant.

Between Egypt and Sinai (under the Abrahamic Covenant), God

only blessed his people, even when they murmured and complained. In fact, from Egypt to Sinai, there is no record of anyone dying!

Why did God stop giving them grace for their egregious attitudes and disobedience? What changed?

It wasn't the people's behavior and it wasn't God's character. It was the covenant the people agreed to in Exodus 19. They essentially said to Moses, "Just tell us what God says to do, and we will do it."

It was prideful of them to claim they would be able to keep God's law, so long as they knew what it was. Under the Law Covenant, they were dependent on their ability. The people hadn't realized yet that what they needed was internal transformation, not external regulation.

When life is chaotic and out of alignment, many people intuitively believe that more laws and rules are the answer to curb behavioral issues.

ON A LIGHTER NOTE

In a certain college, the trustees thought it would be smart to hire the wives of some of the faculty members as they were often well qualified. The plan worked fine, until these wives started getting pregnant. They all wanted to work right up to their delivery day!

The board of trustees made a new rule. The wives could continue teaching until they could no longer pass "the tummy test." They were to face the wall with their toes touching the baseboard, and when their tummies touched the wall, they had to quit.

The wives accepted the rule, but they insisted that it apply to male faculty members as well. As a result, they lost five professors and three department heads.

THE LAW'S EFFECT

Many believe that if we taught more about God's law, then it would curb, if not put an end, to sinful behavior.

Not only does the law not help deter sin, it actually has the opposite effect on our sinful behavior. Leading our lives with the law is like spraying gasoline on a fire in an attempt to extinguish it.

This may seem counter-intuitive, but the Apostle Paul actually declared that the strength of sin is the law (1 Corinthians 15:56). He explained that the purpose of the law was actually to show the Jewish nation that they could not keep it, and reveal to them their need for a Savior.

Many Christians today are still living as if they are under the law, thinking that keeping the commandments is what it's all about. Some people believe that the message of grace and forgiveness will give people a license to sin and keep on sinning because they know that they are forgiven. Scripture indicates the opposite: it is not grace that stirs up sin, but rather, the law.

Have you noticed that the more you try to keep the law, the worse your behavior becomes? And, when you don't keep the law, guilt and condemnation often come calling.

LITTLE RULE BREAKER

Growing up, my parents had a rule at Christmastime that we could not peek at the wrapped presents under the Christmas tree.

For the first five years of my life, I never peeked at a package. But, when I was five years old, one gift under the tree looked like it could be a G.I. Joe action figure. I wanted a G.I. Joe so much that I did the unthinkable. While no one was looking, I pulled back the wrapping paper on that box and looked.

I got so excited! The G.I. Joe was just what I wanted! Shortly after, though, my feelings of elation abated and I started experiencing strong feelings of guilt and shame. I had broken the honor code of, "Thou shalt not peek at your presents."

Now that I had broken the rule, I would need to cover up my

transgression by hiding any evidence of package tampering. _
I would have to restore the wrapping paper so it would appear
untouched by small human hands. Secondly, I would have to deceive
my parents by acting surprised when I unwrapped my G.I. Joe.

My guilt, shame, and deception cast a gloomy shadow over
the excitement of that Christmas morning. My conscience was
obviously very sensitive to my perceived wrongdoing and the
ongoing complications of covering it up. Of course, now I realize
that package-peeking is not a terrible sin, but even this minor offense
cost me carefree joy.

The point is, sin will take you further than you wanted to go,
keep you longer than you wanted to stay, and cost you more than
you were willing to pay. However, for believers in Christ, sin will
not have dominion over us, because we are not under the law, but
under grace.

When we put ourselves under the law, we will find ourselves
dealing with accusation, which often turns into condemnation. We
are called to put our trust and focus on Jesus, who is our life. Living
under the law never leads to life.

DEFENDING FREEDOM FROM LAW

When the path to salvation through Jesus Christ was opened
for the Gentiles (anyone who is not of Jewish descent), there was
serious debate about how the Gentiles would be discipled. To further
complicate the situation, the Jews typically did not have high regard
for Gentiles, and that would be putting it mildly.

The reason discipling the Gentiles was such a sensitive issue is
because the Jews had been practicing the Law for approximately
1,600 years before Christ was born. The law and their traditions were
firmly entrenched into every aspect of their lives!

The root of the Hebrew term used to refer to Jewish law,
"Halakhah," means go or walk. "Halakhah" then, was the way Jews

were directed to behave in every aspect of life. This encompassed civil, criminal, and religious law.

The foundation of Judaism is the Torah (the first five books of the Hebrew Bible). "Torah" means instruction or teaching, and like all teaching, it requires interpretation and application.

The news that Gentiles were now being included in salvation through faith in Christ was absolutely shocking to the Jews. The believers who were still dedicated to keeping the law had some very strong convictions regarding how the Gentiles should live.

But then some of the believers who belonged to the sect of the Pharisees stood up and insisted that the Gentile converts must be circumcised and required to follow the law of Moses. (Acts 15:5)

AN EPIC JOYFUL DECISION

Peter challenged the statement by the Pharisees with a clear and convincing question, followed by the direct truth of saving grace:

> "So why are you now challenging God by burdening the Gentile believers with a yoke that neither we nor our ancestors were able to bear? We believe that we are all saved the same way, by the undeserved grace of the Lord Jesus."
> Acts 15:10-11 NLT

I love that Peter recognized the law for what it was to the Gentiles: a burdensome list of requirements that had now been fulfilled through Jesus Christ. Peter comes to this brilliant conclusion:

> "...And so my judgment is that we should not make it difficult for the Gentiles who are turning to God."
> Acts 15:19 NLT

What a great scripture for us to remember when people come to Christ! Our job is not to load new believers down with all that they should or should not be doing.

Paul explained to the Gentiles the following:

"For it seemed good to the Holy Spirit and to us to lay no greater burden on you than these few requirements: You must abstain from eating food offered to idols, from consuming blood or the meat of strangled animals, and from sexual immorality. If you do this, you will do well. Farewell."
Acts 15:28-29

Following the guidance of the Holy Spirit, they were able to go from 660 laws to just three requirements. The first two requirements were to assist and enhance unity with their fellow Jewish believers. The Jews had long-term, serious convictions regarding eating food offered to idols and consuming blood. The third requirement was to abstain from sexual immorality, which was very prevalent among the Gentiles.

What a great relief for Gentile believers! They would not be subjected to the exhausting laws and traditions which would have required them to change every part of their lives. Gentile men were particularly excited that their salvation would not require surgery!

And there was great joy throughout the church that day as they read this encouraging message.
Acts 15:31 NLT

There is so much confusion swirling around the law and who it applies to. Paul settled the questioning surrounding the law:

"For sin shall not have dominion over you, for you are not under law but under grace." Romans 6:14

Let me be clear, we are not saved by the law, kept by the law or managed by the law. As believers, we are to have nothing to do with the law. The Kingdom of God runs by grace, not the law. The law manifests in many forms. "The law" is anything you must do to merit favor or avoid condemnation.

How awesome that the believers would be able to serve God and grow in him without trying to perfectly perform copious burdensome laws and traditions!

We could boil it all down to this: "We were never meant to be under the law in the first place."

FOUR

THE NEW COVENANT

"The law condemns the best of us; but grace saves the worst of us." - Joseph Prince

The New Covenant is nothing like the Old Covenant. The Old Covenant causes us to look at ourselves; the New Covenant causes us to look to Christ, who was crucified for us.

The scriptures portray the stark contrast between the Old Covenant and the New Covenant in the following comparisons:

The first miracle of Moses (who represents the Law) was to turn water into blood, resulting in death. The first miracle of Jesus (who represents grace) was to turn water into wine, resulting in the celebration of life.

Moses, the Law-giver, was not permitted to lead Israel into the Promised Land. Joshua, whose name means savior, led Israel triumphantly into the Promised Land.

On the first Pentecost, the Law was given on Mount Sinai and 3,000 Israelites died. On the day of Pentecost following the death and resurrection of Jesus, the Spirit was poured out on believers and 3,000 Israelites were saved that day.

The conclusion of the contrasting covenants is undeniable. The Apostle Paul emphatically stated,

> He has made us competent as ministers of a new covenant—not of the letter but of the Spirit; for the letter kills, but the Spirit gives life.
> 2 Corinthians 3:6 NIV

The Word of God is clear, the Old Covenant must go so that the New Covenant can come.

IT IS FINISHED

> So when Jesus had received the sour wine, He said, "It is finished!" And bowing His head, He gave up His spirit.
> John 19:30

It is finished, in the Greek is "tetelestai," which is the same word that means "paid in full."

Jesus paid in full for all time the sins guilt shame for all mankind. Tetelestai was used in an accounting term, which indicates a debt was paid. The uniqueness about the way it was written is that the tense of the word indicates both a point in time it was complete and that it would also continue to be complete or finished.

> "And when Jesus had cried out again in a loud voice, he gave up his spirit. At that moment the curtain of the temple was torn in two from top to bottom...."
> Matthew 27:50-51 NIV

What was finished? Jesus had not yet been buried; had not yet been raised from the dead; had not yet sat down at the right hand of the Father.

The moment he uttered those climactic words, the curtain in the temple was torn in two, signifying the end of the Old Covenant era.

In the Jewish temple, the veil served as the barrier to the Holy of Holies. The Holy of Holies was said to be where God's presence rested and it housed the Ark of the Covenant. Only the high priest could enter this area, and then only one time per year, to make atonement for the sins of Israel (Exodus 30:10).

The message of the veil was that there could be no direct access to God for Israelites. It was like a huge sign which declared No admittance...no trespassing.

The enormous sixty-foot high, four-inch thick curtain was torn in half, and the tear was from top to bottom, from Heaven to earth, clearly indicating the destruction was not man-made, but came from God.

The torn veil announced that because of Jesus substitutionary death on the cross every believer has direct access to God.

By the shedding of his blood and breaking of his body, Jesus was introducing a new superior covenant which qualifies every person to stand as a new creation in Christ before God the Father.

This New Covenant was made between God the Father and Jesus, his Son, on behalf of all mankind. We who are in Christ reap the benefits as beneficiaries of this amazing New Covenant!

GOOD NEWS

It's essential for us to understand that the benefits of this New Covenant don't depend on our faithfulness, but on the faithfulness of God. Under the law, our actions are pivotal to our outcomes; under grace, our outcomes rest in God's goodness and our role is to believe and receive his blessings.

Here is the main clause of the New Covenant:

> But this is the new covenant **I will** make with the people of Israel on that day, says the Lord: **I will** put my laws in their minds, and **I will** write them on their hearts. **I will** be their God, and they will be my people. And **I will** forgive their wickedness, and **I will** never again remember their sins.
> Hebrews 8:10,12 NLT (emphasis added)

Notice all of the "I will" statements that God makes in this passage. He is communicating the New Covenant order.

The following is a portion of the message that Paul preached everywhere he ministered:

> "Therefore, my friends, I want you to know that through Jesus the forgiveness of sins is proclaimed to you. Through him everyone who believes is set free from every sin, a justification you were not able to obtain under the law of Moses."
> Acts 13:38-39 NIV

This passage that the Apostle Paul preached at Antioch deserves our earnest attention. Through Jesus, forgiveness from every sin is proclaimed. Through him, everyone who believes is set free from every sin.

It gets even better! Not only are we forgiven and set free from every sin, we are also justified. The word "justified" means that we have been declared righteous by God.

Why is it so important for us to understand the complete forgiveness of our past, present, and future sins?

Many believers struggle to believe that future sins are forgiven as well. Consider this question: when Jesus died on the cross securing our forgiveness, how many of those sins were future sins? Unless you're over 2,000 years old, all our sins were future sins.

It was difficult for me to grasp this truth having been taught that we are responsible for getting our sins under the blood by our confession of sin. Our inability to effectively mediate this essential aspect of our salvation opens the door to confusion and condemnation.

This doesn't mean we will never need to repent of our actions or attitudes. In fact, dialog with our Heavenly Father is often needed and appropriate as we navigate difficulties regarding our behavior. However, It does mean that we will be thanking God for his forgiveness, not trying to obtain it through our own efforts.

If you and I don't have confidence that all of our sins have been forgiven, then we lack confidence to enjoy the wonderful standing that we have in him. When we believe that we need to do something to earn, deserve, or secure the forgiveness of God, the good news becomes less good.

ON A LIGHTER SIDE

This reminds me of a "Dennis the Menace" cartoon I once saw. In the comic strip, Dennis and his little friend, Joey, are pictured walking home from a visit with their neighbor, Mrs. Wilson, the Grandmotherly epitome of sweetness.

As Dennis and Joey walk away from Mrs. Wilson's house with as many cookies as they can possibly carry, Joey asks, "Dennis, I wonder what we did to deserve all these cookies?" Dennis responds, "Ah Joey, you don't get it. Mrs. Wilson doesn't bake us cookies because we're nice. She bakes us cookies because she's nice."

If you understand that cartoon, you have a basic understanding of what grace is all about. God doesn't love us based on our goodness or perfection; he loves us based on his nature. He doesn't love us because we are good; he loves us because he is good and his love is the essence of what grace is all about. His mercy and his kindness are freely given to us! In fact, when we were at our very worst, God gave us his very best.

Here is an acronym for grace to help us better understand it:

God's
Riches
At
Christ's
Expense

Having received the free gift of eternal life, we truly have received God's riches at Christ's expense. We have been given forgiveness, cleansing, eternal life, the Holy Spirit to dwell within us, and so much more!

The gospel is free, but it didn't come cheap. God's grace toward us cost Jesus more than we will ever know. Jesus took upon himself the sins, guilt, shame, and sickness of all mankind so that we might experience, what I call, the great exchange: our sins and judgment, in exchange for his forgiveness and righteousness.

The word "gospel" means good news. The Greek word, "euangelion," means nearly-too-good-to-be-true news. The word "euangelion" was rarely used before the scriptures came along because, well, there wasn't much news that was nearly-too-good-to-be-true. That changed when Christ came! The writers of the New Testament used this word seventy-six times!

Unfortunately, in most Christian circles, we have unknowingly followed teachings that have made the good news less good. This statement sounds harsh and perhaps offensive, but I believe this claim can be substantiated.

CONFESSION OBSESSION

I went to a very good Bible college that had wonderful

professors who passionately taught the Bible and modeled strong moral character. I will always be thankful for my professors and the education I received!

Unfortunately, we were also introduced to a number of teachings that are incongruent with the good news. For instance, we were taught to confess every sin because any unconfessed sin is unforgiven sin. We were also taught that our sin creates separation with God.

The scripture to substantiate this separation was Isaiah 59:2, which states:

> But your iniquities have separated you from your God;
> and your sins have hidden His face from you.

That's fairly heavy. Add to that Psalm 66:18 where David said:

> If I regard iniquity in my heart, the Lord will not hear me.

I was zealous to confess my sins because I wanted to stay in relationship with Jesus and have my prayers answered! This was no small task because, according to this teaching, we could not cherry pick which sins to confess. We needed to confess all sin, which included:

- sins of commission (things I should not have done)
- sins of omission (things that I should have done, but didn't)
- sins of thought life
- sins of wrong motivations
- sins of whatever is not of faith

We were taught to spend time waiting for the Holy Spirit to clearly reveal every sin that we needed to confess so we would not be separated from God.

Looking back, the amount of time I spent trying to remember

every possible sin in order to stay in fellowship with my Heavenly Father makes me sad. There was always something more to get right in order to be right with God! I was certainly more sin conscious than God conscious. Does this sound like a wonderful way to live?

My earthly Father never treated me like this. He didn't require me to confess every wrong to him in order for us to stay in relationship with him. As a father and a grandfather myself, there is no way that I would want my children or grandchildren to spend copious amounts of time trying to figure out how they might have offended me during the day.

This is what I mean when I say that we can make the good news less good. So where is the problem, and how do we solve it?

When the Father looks at you, he doesn't see anything wrong. He's not obsessed by sin; he is consumed by life!

When we study scripture, we need to ask the simple question: under which covenant was it spoken? If we are drawing from two covenants, the mixture will be a mess.

FIVE

THE MESS WITH MIXTURE

"The Law was never given to gentiles, but to Jews. So, why do so many gentiles struggle today with mixing law and grace?" -John Paul Warren

M ost believers don't comprehend the essential nature of covenants, nor the serious danger of covenant mixture. Unlike fashionable clothing, biblical covenants were never created to mix and match.

Isaiah wrote that our sins separate us from God:

But your iniquities have separated you from your God; and your sins have hidden His face from you, so that He will not hear.
Isaiah 59:2

In contrast, the Apostle Paul wrote that nothing can separate us from God:

No power in the sky above or in the earth below—indeed, nothing in all creation will ever be able to separate us from the love of God that is revealed in Christ Jesus our Lord.
Romans 8:39 NLT

Which was correct?

Isaiah was correct, living under the Old Covenant, addressing people under the Old Covenant. Paul was also correct, living under the New Covenant, speaking to people under the New Covenant.

What about the condition of our hearts?

Jeremiah wrote:

The human heart is the most deceitful of all things, and desperately wicked. Who really knows how bad it is?
Jeremiah 17:9 NLT

Apostle Paul later wrote:

But God be thanked that though you were slaves of sin, yet you obeyed from the heart that form of doctrine to which you were delivered.
Romans 6:17

So, do we have a deceitful and wicked heart? Or, can we be obedient from the heart?

The deceitful and wicked heart Jeremiah wrote of was true for those living under the Old Covenant. Likewise, the obedient heart Paul wrote of was true for believers living under the New Covenant.

You might be wondering how the New Covenant is like the Old Covenant.

It isn't! Notice the numerous contrasts between Law and Grace:

Law	Grace
Given by Moses	Came through Jesus
Reveals what we need to do	Reveals what God has done
Letter kills	Spirit gives life
Demands righteousness	Provides righteousness
Old wineskin	New wine
Sins remembered	Sins forgiven
Blessings and cursing	Dispenses only blessings
What you must do	What Jesus has done
Disqualified by disobedience	Qualified by Jesus
Ministry of death & condemnation	Ministry of life & justification

This side-by-side comparison shows how important it is to understand which covenant we're under. When Old Covenant scriptures are applied to New Covenant people, not only does it create confusion, but also, a loss of New Covenant power.

WHEN IS ENOUGH, ENOUGH?

There is a well-worn page in my Bible where I often turned to remind folks to do more for God in order to receive his blessing:

"...if My people who are called by My name will humble themselves, and pray and seek My face, and turn from their wicked ways, then I will hear from heaven, and will forgive their sin and heal their land."
2 Chronicles 7:14

When I used to preach this message at my church, I would focus on our human responsibility to do more: pray more; fast more; repent more; be more humble!

The message I preached weighed me down. When I fasted and prayed for three days, afterward, I felt condemned that I had not fasted for five days. When I prayed for one hour, I would often feel that I had disappointed God by not praying longer.

I no longer turn to this verse to teach on how we need to do more for God because it is Old Covenant. Many Christians love this verse, but it actually doesn't directly apply to those of us who live under the New Covenant.

You see, while all scripture is for us, not all scripture was written to us. When examined, we discover that God is addressing "my people, called by my name." Under the Old Covenant, this meant the Jews.

It then proceeds into the if/then conditions for fulfillment: if his people would humble themselves, pray, seek his face, and turn from their wicked ways, then he would hear from Heaven, forgive their sin, and heal their land.

Old Covenant agreements are conditional: God would do his part if-and-when his people did their part. New Covenant is about what God has done and how he has provided us with all things that pertain to life and Godliness.

HOUDINI MET HIS MATCH

Houdini, the great escape artist, claimed that he could escape from any jail cell in the world in less than an hour, provided he could go into the cell dressed in his street clothes. Every time he was given the challenge, he accepted and did just as he promised. He was left alone in a locked cell, and within a few short minutes, he would miraculously escape.

A small town in the British Isles built a new jail cell they were very proud of and encouraged Houdini to give it a try. Houdini agreed to take their challenge!

As they closed Houdini's jail cell, he took off his coat and set to work with his lock pick.

For thirty minutes, Houdini worked feverishly, getting nowhere. After an hour had passed, his confident expression completely disappeared. Something was so unusual about this lock!

After two hours, Houdini literally collapsed against the door in exhaustion and the door swung open. That's when he first discovered the reason he could not pick this lock: it had never been locked at all. Houdini was frustrated and exhausted in trying to unlock an unlocked door.

In a similar way, I'm convinced that a large percentage of believers are frustrated trying to get forgiveness and blessings from God, that He has already provided for them.

NEW WINE IN NEW WINESKINS

"And no one puts new wine into old wineskins; or else the new wine will burst the wineskins and be spilled, and the wineskins will be ruined. But new wine must be put into new wineskins, and both are preserved."
Luke 5:37-38

Jesus spoke of new wineskins. When new wine is poured into an old wineskin, the old skin is unable to handle the expansion that takes place during the fermentation process. The old wineskin bursts and both are lost in the process!

Jesus gave this analogy to let us know that the Law of the Old Testament and the grace of the New Testament were never meant to mix. Wine, being a type of the Holy Spirit, is meant to dwell in believers who have become new wineskins, also known as new creations in Jesus Christ.

TIME TO LEAVE BABYLON

In 597 BC, Israel was deported to the city of Babylon. The name "Babylon" is from the Hebrew word "Babel," which means confusion by mixing. The word originates from after the great flood when people stopped on the plains of Shinar to build a tower that could reach heaven. They were unified in their efforts to make a name for themselves.

In order to disrupt their self-glorifying efforts, God sent a mixture of languages:

"Come, let Us go down and there confuse their language, that they may not understand one another's speech." So the Lord scattered them abroad from there over the face of all the earth, and they ceased building the city.
Genesis 11:7-8

Living our lives mixing law and grace will lead to bondage and confusion. The mixture will also dilute the power of the gospel of Jesus Christ in our lives. We were never meant to trust our own behavior to deserve, earn, or merit favor with God. We were created to enjoy the blessings and favor of the Lord through the unearned, undeserved, unmerited grace of God.

After seventy years in captivity, Israel came out of their Babylonian bondage. The church of the living God has experienced the bondage of mixture for far too long! It is time for the church to come out of

Babylon; out of the confusion of mixing Law and Grace.

The New Covenant order in the following passage beautifully captures the truth that God is the one who initiates and orchestrates every part of our salvation! Our part is to believe and receive the free gift of eternal life in Christ.

> ...and through him God reconciled everything to himself. He made peace with everything in heaven and on earth by means of Christ's blood on the cross. This includes you who were once far away from God. You were his enemies, separated from him by your evil thoughts and actions. Yet now he has reconciled you to himself through the death of Christ in his physical body. As a result, he has brought you into his own presence, and you are holy and blameless as you stand before him without a single fault. Colossians 1:22 NLT

Can you see the night-and-day difference between New Covenant Grace and Old Covenant Law? Why would we ever go back to the Old Covenant Law which was abolished at the cross?

This New Covenant is not a covenant we have made with God. It is based on God the Father making a covenant with God the Son. Our position in Christ brings us into the place of being beneficiaries of a perfect covenant made by the perfect Father and Son.

SIX

SIN-CONSCIOUS OR GOD-CONSCIOUS?

"When the Father looks at you, He doesn't see anything wrong. He's not obsessed by sin; He's not like us. He is consumed by life!" - Graham Cooke

In my youth, I didn't understand that forgiveness was based on the perfection of the sacrifice of Jesus Christ once and for all.

No doubt, any teaching that subjects us to condemnation is not from God but is, in fact, a trap of the enemy!

Sir Robert Watson-Watt, the Scotsman who invented radar, was rewarded 140,000 dollars, the highest award ever earned for a wartime invention. Years later, while driving in Canada, he was caught in a radar trap and arrested for speeding. He wrote the following poem about it:

Pity Sir Robert Watson-Watt,
strange target of his radar plot,
and thus with others I can mention,
a victim of his own invention.
His magical all-seeing eye
enabled cloud bound planes to fly,
but now by some ironic twist,
it spots the speeding motorist
and bites, no doubt with legal wit,
the hand that once created it!

A radar trap is most effective when it's not detected by sight. Most believers don't recognize teachings that actually open the door to accusations that lead to condemnation. No doubt, teachings that lead us to focus on guilt, shame and sin consciousness are a trap of the enemy to rob us of confidence, joy, peace, and security in our relationship with God.

The name "Satan" means the Accuser. When we mix law into our lives, we open the door to Satan to bring accusation and condemnation.

By the way, the Apostle Paul referred to the law as the ministry of death and condemnation (2 Corinthians 3:7,9).

RECOGNIZE THE ENEMIES STRATEGY

Have you ridden the carousel at the carnival? 'Round and round it goes, up and down, playing the same loud, obnoxious music over and over again. There's a lot of movement, but the scenery never changes because in reality, it's going nowhere.

The enemy's strategy is to get you to ride his carousel of accusation!

Why did you say that?
You will never amount to anything.

You're not smart enough.
Everyone thinks you're a loser.
You don't follow through!
Even God is mad at you. In fact, he's given up on you.
You've blown it too many times. God is not going to forgive
you this time. You're lazy and unproductive, and no one
wants to be your friend.
Even your parents don't believe in you.

Like the carousel, he keeps thoughts like these cycling through your brain.

His methods haven't changed because they've proven to be effective. Satan's strategy is to inundate your thinking with lies and half truths so he can claim real estate in your mind. His goal is to get you to shake hands with the lie and come into agreement with his deception until it becomes a part of your belief system.

Adding your own confession of the enemy's lies to this will bring you into bondage. It's from that vantage point that fear, anxiety, doubt, unbelief, and despair converge to debilitate and derail you from your God-given destiny.

Thank God we have been given mighty weapons of warfare to overcome every attack of the wicked one. The Apostle Paul wrote:

For although we live in the natural realm, we don't wage a military campaign employing human weapons, using manipulation to achieve our aims. Instead, our spiritual weapons are energized with divine power to effectively dismantle the defenses behind which people hide. We can demolish every deceptive fantasy that opposes God and break through every arrogant attitude that is raised up in defiance of the true knowledge of God. We capture, like prisoners of war, every thought and insist that it bow in obedience to the Anointed One.

2 Corinthians 10:3-5 TPT

Our thoughts must keep us out of the enemy's POW camp! By casting down those defeating thoughts and aligning our thinking with the Word of God, we reverse the curse and embrace the truth which sets us free.

People often say "the truth will set you free." Actually, it's the truth that you know and embrace that will bring freedom into your life.

> Jesus said to those Jews who believed in him, "When you continue to embrace all that I teach, you prove that you are my true followers. For if you embrace the truth, it will release true freedom into your lives."
> John 8:31-32 TPT

BOLDNESS TO APPROACH GOD

The belief that we have to get right with God before we can come to him is a religious tradition that hinders us from coming to God with confidence.

It goes against the teachings of the New Covenant where we are encouraged to come to

Jesus as we are. On the contrary, the religious teaching seems to instruct you to clean yourself up before you take a shower.

The writer of Hebrews says:

> Let us therefore come boldly to the throne of grace, that we may obtain mercy and find grace to help in time of need.
> Hebrews 4:16

Coming boldly to the throne of grace shows confidence in our right standing before God. The New Covenant is all about the grace of God, and this grace is not merely teaching or topic. Grace is the person of Jesus Christ manifesting his love and his life to us.

In the Old Testament, when a man sinned, he would make a sin offering, which was usually a lamb. The priest would examine the lamb to make sure it had no blemish or imperfection. Please note that the priest examined the lamb, not the man. The man was not asked to disrobe for the priest to check for imperfections.

The same is true for us under the New Covenant. God does not examine us for sin! He examines our sacrifice, who is Jesus. Great news! The Lamb of God is perfect in every way!

Under the Old Covenant, the man would lay his hand on the head of the lamb with the implication that his sins were transferred to the lamb. Next, the lamb had to be killed to atone for the sins that were transferred to it. For the lamb's part, I'm quite sure it didn't go to its death willingly.

On the other hand, Jesus chose to die on the cross for our sins so we might be completely forgiven, redeemed, and set free.

He who knew no sin became sin for us that we might be made the righteousness of God in Christ Jesus.
2 Corinthians 5:21

Please allow your new identity in Christ to sink in. You are no longer a mere sinner saved by grace. You are forgiven; cleansed; a new creation in Christ. You are the righteousness of God in Christ Jesus.

This makes some believers uncomfortable because they have a hard time believing that they are now righteous in God's sight. I understand! This gospel is such good news that sometimes it's hard to believe it!

Under the Old Covenant, the blood of the animal could only provide a temporary covering for sin. Every time the man failed, he had to bring another sacrifice which would be offered by the priest. In contrast, the blood of Jesus settled it once and for all.

And every priest stands ministering daily and offering
repeatedly the same sacrifices, which can never take away
sins. But this Man, (Jesus) after He had offered one
sacrifice for sins forever, sat down at the right hand of
God...
Hebrews 10:11-12

It's interesting that, of all the items in the tabernacle and later
in the temple, there were no La-Z-Boy recliners where the priests
could sit down and relax. The fact that there was no place for them
to sit implies that their work was never really completed.

The amazing news is:

For by one offering He has perfected forever those who
are being sanctified.
Hebrews 10:14

In addition, the scripture states that we are sanctified, or, made
holy, through Jesus' sacrifice:

By that will we have been sanctified through the offering
of the body of Jesus Christ once for all.
Hebrews 10:10

Our salvation includes the forgiveness of all our past, present,
and future sins.

A TRAGIC MISUNDERSTANDING

If we confess our sins, He is faithful and just to forgive us
our sins and to cleanse us from all unrighteousness.
1 John 1:9

This beautiful New Covenant scripture has been misinterpreted and misused by Bible-believing Christians for generations. The magnitude of the negative impact is very sad and motivates me to expose the misinterpretation for what it is.

One of the first rules for proper interpretation of a scripture is to know the historical context for the particular passage. Knowing the what, where, and how is key to understanding the context in which John is writing this letter.

John wrote this letter at a time when Gnostics were infiltrating the churches. Gnosticism was perhaps the most dangerous heresy that threatened the early church during the first three centuries, influenced by such philosophers as Plato. Gnostics were perceived as a privileged class, elevated by a higher, deeper knowledge of God that they had acquired on a higher plane of existence.

Gnostics of the day asserted that matter is inherently evil and spirit is good. As a result of this presupposition, Gnostics were teaching that anything done in the body (even the grossest sin) had no meaning because real life existed in the spirit realm only, rejecting the biblical teaching of sin.

The Gnostics believed that Jesus' physical body was not real, but only seemed to be physical, and that his spirit descended upon him at his baptism but left him just before his crucifixion. They did not believe Jesus had come in the flesh, and they did not believe in his finished work on the cross.

Typically, John would specifically address who he was speaking to in his letters. In the opening verses of 1 John, it is evident that he is addressing the Gnostics, writing the following:

> That which was from the beginning, which we have heard, which we have seen with our eyes, which we have looked upon, and our hands have handled, concerning the Word of life— the life was manifested, and we have seen, and bear witness, and declare to you that eternal life which was with the Father and was manifested to us - that which we have seen and heard we declare to you...
> 1 John 1:1-2 (emphasis added)

It is abundantly clear through all the physical descriptions John details of his and other's personal interactions with Jesus that he is addressing people who did not believe Jesus had come in the flesh.

John was building a case, using thirteen references in two verses, that Jesus had truly come to them in the flesh.

THE INVITATION

We have seen and heard and declare to you that you also may have fellowship with us; and truly our fellowship is with the Father and with His Son Jesus Christ.
1 John 1:3

The verse you just read is an invitation for Gnostics to come into faith in Christ. Notice the pronouns: "...declare to you, that you also may have fellowship with us, our fellowship is with the Father..."

John also emphatically emphasizes the need for the Gnostics to believe in sin.

If we say that we have no sin, we deceive ourselves, and the truth is not in us. If we say that we have not sinned, we make Him a liar, and His word is not in us.
1 John 1:8,10

In the midst of these statements, 1 John 1:9 is an invitation for them to renounce their unbelief regarding sin and receive the Savior who is faithful and just to forgive all their sins and cleanse them from all unrighteousness.

JOHN ADDRESSING BELIEVERS

It's important to notice that after John finishes addressing the

Gnostics, he identifies that he is writing to believers. In 1 John 2:1, John addresses the believers as "My little children." He went on to say, "My little children, these things I write to you, so that you may not sin. And if anyone sins, we have an Advocate with the Father, Jesus Christ the righteous.

Then, in 1 John 2:12, John states:

> I write to you, little children, because your sins are forgiven you for His name's sake.

John was not telling believers to make sure they confess their sins. Instead, John was pointing them to the finished work of Jesus. He was writing them because their sins are forgiven for his name's sake.

Scripture interprets scripture. We cannot build a doctrine based on one verse. If ongoing confession of sins is essential for forgiveness, then the Apostle Paul, who wrote two thirds of the New Testament, would have written about the necessity of believers to confess their sins to receive forgiveness over and over again. The fact is, he didn't mention it once in all of his letters to the churches.

It wasn't because he was lacking opportunity. For instance, in the Corinthian church, some of the Christian men were going to temple prostitutes in the city. The Apostle Paul did not instruct them to make sure they confessed their sins. Instead, Paul reminded them that they are the temple of the Holy Spirit and that they were bought with a price. He also instructed them that they should glorify God with their bodies and with their spirits, which belong to God (1 Corinthians 6:19-20).

Paul's approach was not to make them sin conscious, but God conscious. He also reminded them that they have been purchased by God for the purpose of glorifying him.

John also reminded us of how continuous, complete, and unencumbered our forgiveness through the blood of Jesus Christ really is.

But if we walk in the light as He is in the light, we have fellowship with one another, and the blood of Jesus Christ His Son cleanses us from all sin.

1 John 1:7

The word "cleanse" in this verse denotes a present continuous action, which means that, from the moment one receives Christ, the blood of Jesus keeps on cleansing. It is like a continuous cascading waterfall of his forgiveness. Even when you fail, this waterfall never stops; it keeps on cleansing.

SEVEN

RED LETTER ALERT

I n order to rightly divide the Word of God, it's important for us to understand that everything in the Bible is written for us, but not all of it was written to us.

From here on out, I'll be using the terms "Old Testament" and "New Testament" interchangeably with "Old Covenant" and "New Covenant." We have ample evidence that many Old Testament teachings are not to be applied to New Testament believers.

You might be surprised to know that my search for untangling scriptures actually includes some that are written in red letters. I'm obviously referring to some of the teaching of Jesus in the gospels.

When we want to know which covenant a verse is under, we typically ask, "When was it spoken?" Most would say Jesus' red-letter words are New Testament teachings because they're recorded in the gospels found at the beginning of the New Testament (the books of Matthew, Mark, Luke, and John).

However, technically, the New Testament cannot be implemented without the atoning blood, and we know that Jesus is the sacrificial Lamb of God for the world. So, the "New Testament" or "New Covenant" wasn't actually activated until Jesus died on the cross. This has an impact on how we view many of Jesus' teachings before the cross.

Consider the following:

Each "New Covenant" must have a death and bloodshed by a sacrifice.

> And for this reason He is the Mediator of the new covenant, by means of death, for the redemption of the transgressions under the first covenant, that those who are called may receive the promise of the eternal inheritance.
> Hebrews 9:15

> The will goes into effect only after the person's death. While the person who made it is still alive, the will cannot be put into effect.
> Hebrews 9:17 NLT

The common consensus is that the gospels are all New Testament teachings that can be directly applied to our lives. This conclusion has caused considerable confusion and misunderstanding in interpreting these scriptures.

The New Testament actually begins in: Matthew 27; Mark 15; Luke 23; and John 19. It's in these four chapters that Jesus dies on the cross, marking the New Covenant.

After Jesus died on the cross, the veil in the temple was torn. That supernatural sign verified the end of the Old Covenant and the beginning of the New Covenant. The New Covenant dramatically changed our access and relationship to God.

> Therefore, brothers and sisters, since we have confidence to enter the Most Holy Place by the blood of Jesus, by

a new and living way opened for us through the curtain, that is, his body, and since we have a great priest over the house of God, let us draw near to God with a sincere heart and with the full assurance that faith brings, having our hearts sprinkled to cleanse us from a guilty conscience and having our bodies washed with pure water.
Hebrews 10:19-22 NIV

The torn curtain also signifies the end of the Old Testament sacrifices, the end of Old Testament priesthood, and the end of the Law Covenant.

In that He says, "A new covenant," He has made the first obsolete. Now what is becoming obsolete and growing old is ready to vanish away.
Hebrews 8:13

However, a majority of Jesus' red-letter words were spoken before the veil had been torn, which indicates that most of his teachings were spoken to Jews who were operating under the law. In fact, many Jewish people continued worshiping in the temple after the veil was torn, continuing to apply their traditions of the priesthood and sacrifices until the old literally vanished away with the destruction of the temple in 70 AD.

JESUS WAS BORN UNDER THE LAW

But when the fullness of time had come, God sent forth His Son, born of a woman, born under the law...
Galatians 4:4

Jesus was born under the law, circumcised by law, and was presented in the temple according to the law. The Jewish people

Jesus interacted with were also under the law.

To those under the law, Jesus said:

> The teachers of the law and the Pharisees sit in Moses'
> seat. So you must be careful to do everything they tell
> you.
> Matthew 23:2-3a NIV

The above passage affirms that Jesus was instructing the Jews according to the Old Covenant.

Consider another scripture written to those living under the law:

> But I tell you that anyone who is angry with a brother
> or sister will be subject to judgment. Again, anyone who
> says to a brother or sister, 'Raca,' is answerable to the
> court. And anyone who says, 'You fool!' will be in danger
> of the fire of hell.
> Matthew 5:22 NIV

Jesus said this to Jewish people under the law and it is clearly not good news, because God's grace is glaringly absent.

Everything that Jesus said was true, but not everything he said was true for you. It's very important for us to examine the context of His words to know who He is speaking to. Jesus called the Pharisees serpents, brood of vipers, sons of hell and hypocrites. Thankfully those names were not spoken to us as sons and daughters of God.

It would be a huge mistake for us to dismiss the pre-cross teachings of Jesus by saying that they are just for people under the Old Covenant. There are many wonderful treasures in these teachings of Jesus that are applicable for our lives. In 2 Timothy 3:16 we are instructed:

> All Scripture is given by inspiration of God, and is
> profitable for doctrine, for reproof, for correction, for
> instruction in righteousness...

Jesus gave grace to sinners and law to the self righteous. Jesus is a wonderful physician, giving people exactly what they need.

The law is only good news for perfect people, but there was only one of those who has ever lived on this planet.

Jesus, being a Jewish man, was committed to the Sabbath, Jewish festivals, and the fulness of Jewish life. When Jesus cleansed lepers, he told them to go to the priest to be examined according to the law.

When the rich young ruler came to Jesus and asked him, "What must I do to inherit eternal life?" Jesus gave the young ruler the answer of the law because he was still under the law.

> You know the commandments: 'Do not commit adultery,' 'Do not steal,' 'Do not murder,' 'Do not bear false witness,' 'Do not defraud,' 'Honor your father and your mother.'
> Mark 10:19

There is nothing wrong with this, because Jesus was born under the law to redeem those under the law.

THE LAW GOES TO A PRISTINE LEVEL

Jesus made a number of statements that were meant to raise the bar of the law from physical actions to thoughts, motives, and intentions of the heart.

> "You have heard that it has been said, 'thou shall not commit adultery.' But I say unto you if you look upon a woman to lust after her, you have committed adultery already in your heart."
> Matthew 5:27

Jesus is quoting the law that was given to the nation of Israel regarding adultery.

Jesus raises the level of the law, because one of the primary purposes of the law was to bring Jewish people to the realization that they could not keep the law. It was meant to prepare them to receive the Savior of the world.

Jesus said:

> "For if you forgive men their trespasses, your heavenly Father will also forgive you. But if you do not forgive men their trespasses, neither will your Father forgive your trespasses."
> Matthew 6:14-15

This popular verse spoken by Jesus has all the earmarks of the law. It's not comforting to hear that our forgiveness from our heavenly Father rests on our ability to forgive others. Not only is this not good news, it's downright bad news because most of us are inept at forgiving others. What if we forget to forgive someone? Or, what if we thought we forgave someone, but the next time we see them it becomes obvious we had not really forgiven them.

Many Christians find themselves conflicted because they believe that if they have any vestige of unforgiveness in their heart, they are not forgiven.

This conditional scripture is regularly used in churches, but it's not actually written to New Testament believers. Remember, Jesus was speaking this to Jewish people who were still under the law.

Under the New Covenant, we are not still trying to qualify for forgiveness. We have been forgiven!

Still, many of us do not live this way. Because of the mixture of covenants that I was once taught, I used to spend copious amounts of time and energy trying to obtain forgiveness.

Apostle Paul, speaking from the New Covenant, gives us the appropriate perspective:

> ...be kind to one another, tenderhearted, forgiving one

another, even as God in Christ forgave you.
Ephesians 4:32

It's essential to notice the past tense used in this verse: forgiving one another, even as God in Christ forgave you.

Consider the contrast:

Old Covenant: Forgive – in order to be forgiven
New Covenant: Forgive – as Christ has forgiven you

This verse indicates that we are ministering to others from a position of already having been forgiven.

Under the law, forgiveness is something to be obtained; under grace, forgiveness is something God has already given. Forgiveness is a gift, and in Christ, we have received it.

Jesus fulfilled the law on the cross, and after the cross, he changed his message. On the night he rose from the dead, Jesus began preaching unconditional forgiveness.

> And he said, "Yes, it was written long ago that the Messiah would suffer and die and rise from the dead on the third day. It was also written that this message would be proclaimed in the authority of his name to all the nations, beginning in Jerusalem: 'There is forgiveness of sins for all who repent."
> Luke 24:46-47 NLT

AM I RIGHTEOUS ENOUGH?

I remember becoming fearful as a new Christian reading Matthew 5:20 where Jesus said, "For I tell you that unless your righteousness surpasses that of the Pharisees and the teachers of the law, you will certainly not enter the kingdom of God." I processed this red-letter verse as a New Testament scripture that was for me.

The law tends to leave you wondering, "Am I good enough?" "Have I done enough?" "Am I saved?" But on the other hand, grace gives us the confidence to say, "Jesus has done it all." "Jesus is good enough." "Jesus qualified me through his finished work on the cross."

Because I was mixing covenants, I became performance oriented like the Pharisees who fasted twice a week and tithed to God even what came out of their gardens. I assumed I had to perform at an even higher level than this, or else I would not enter into the Kingdom of God!

As a new believer, it's no wonder I wrestled with fear, guilt, and condemnation when I didn't perform at a high level of spirituality. Perhaps you can imagine all the unintended tangling of fear, guilt, shame, confusion, and condemnation I experienced from trying to live under the Old Covenant as a New Covenant believer?

It's imperative that we understand that the New Covenant doesn't begin until the cross. Jesus was clearly living under the law to fulfill the law, and to redeem those under the law.

IN TRANSITION

Jesus lived between two covenants as our representative. He came to fulfill the old law so that we might relate to God through a new and better covenant which was purchased by his blood.

I realize that changing our thinking regarding some of the teachings of Jesus can be shocking and even unsettling. Having our paradigms changed from the old to the new can be compared to doing a delicate dance in a minefield.

My references to the ministry of Jesus to people under the Old Covenant are never meant to diminish him or his wonderful plan. My purpose is to bring covenant clarity where covenant confusion has reigned unabated.

To be clear, Jesus taught many things that are to us and for us.

For instance, when he said "I am the way, the truth and the life, no man comes to the Father except through me" (John 14:6), it was applicable to both Old and New Covenant believers.

Perhaps it would be beneficial for me to highlight the many ways that Jesus was in the process of transitioning and preparing people to move from the Old Covenant to the New Covenant.

JESUS DOES NOT FIT IN A BOX

Throughout his earthly ministry, Jesus was full of grace and truth. The way he loved and reached out to sinners bore no resemblance to the rigid, law-keeping Pharisees.

Jesus' first miracle was to turn 150 gallons of water into wine at a marriage celebration. This miracle had nothing to do with saving lives! The groom had not provided enough wine for the wedding celebration, so Jesus provided the wine instead. This miracle brought the groom great dignity within his community and also brought glory to God.

Jesus went out of his way to visit a Samaritan woman by a well. She had been married five times and was presently living with a man that was not her husband. Not only did he reveal to her that he was the Messiah; he chose her to become an effective messenger to her village. Following her surprising encounter with Jesus at the well, she immediately went to other Samaritans to testify and encourage them to receive this man named Jesus who seemed to know everything about her.

Jesus regularly violated the religious traditions of the hypocritical Pharisees and Sadducees, or, as I like to call them, the Wouldn't-sees and the Couldn't-sees of his day.

JESUS REVEALED HIMSELF

After Jesus' death on the cross, two of Jesus' disciples were walking together on the road to Emmaus, talking about everything that had happened.

Jesus himself actually came up and walked along with them but they did not recognize him. When Jesus asked them what they were talking about, one of them asked, "Are you the only one visiting Jerusalem who does not know the things that have happened there in these days?"

Jesus asked them, "What things?" (Luke 24:17-19)

They explained how Jesus had been crucified, and how the women had seen angels, but his body was gone.

Jesus said to them:

> "How foolish you are, and how slow you are to believe all that the prophets have spoken. Did not the Messiah have to suffer these things and then enter his glory?" And beginning with Moses and all the prophets, he explained to them what was said about Him in all the scriptures concerning Himself.
> Luke 24:26 NIV

Jesus gave them a comprehensive Bible study that included types of himself throughout the Old Testament! He wasn't talking to them about Moses and the prophets so that they would have a better understanding of Moses and the prophets; he was talking to them about Moses and the prophets so they would have a better understanding of why he came.

After this, Jesus revealed himself to them through the breaking of bread, then he disappeared. Jesus had given them such amazing revelation into his involvement in the Old Testament that they actually discussed how their hearts were burning within them on the road while Jesus was teaching them.

It's clear through this story and throughout the gospels that much of what Jesus communicated was intended for Jews who were under the law. That fact doesn't in any way diminish who Jesus is and what he has done.

When we study scripture, Old Testament and New, wisdom invites us to learn to discern the truths that directly apply to us as New Testament believers. The scriptures don't simply exist to teach us how to live our lives, although that does happen. We don't just read the scriptures to gain knowledge of God, although that's great. We don't mainly study the Word to get motivated or inspired, though this will also occur.

The essential motivation to read and study the Bible is to have a personal encounter with the Living Christ. Our highest goal is not to know the book of the Lord, but to know the Lord of the book.

EIGHT

WELCOME HOLY SPIRIT

"We have been given the privilege to host this presence. The Holy Spirit is in me for my sake but he is upon me for yours." - Bill Johnson

A couple went to a garage sale and bought a little bowl about five inches in diameter for three dollars. They liked it enough to put it on their mantle in their living room. After seven years, they decided to have it appraised.

Experts identified the bowl as a 1,000-year-old Chinese "Ding" which is from the Northern Song Dynasty. They consigned the bowl for auction. It was estimated to sell for between $200,000 and $300,000. However, a London dealer paid $2,225,000 for it at the auction in New York City.

Can you imagine the difference in their care for the ancient bowl after they received the overwhelming epiphany regarding its extravagant value? They must have been extremely careful with their precious bowl. The little bowl hadn't suddenly increased in worth. What had changed was their revelation of the little bowl's immense value.

In this same way, the more revelation we have of Holy Spirit, the greater we will love and value his ministry in us and through us. How could we ever put a value on Holy Spirit? He is beyond description in who he is and what he does.

Here are a number of the things Holy Spirit does:

He helps us to be built up
He helps us to abound in hope
He leads us into all truth
He reveals things to come
He glorifies Jesus
He reminds us what Jesus taught
He transforms us into Christ's character
He gives us spiritual gifts
He clothes us with power to be a witness
He communes with us
He loves us
Righteousness peace and joy comes through Holy Spirit
He helps us to pray
He intercedes through us

Why do so many believers leave Holy Spirit on the mantle or treat him as an impersonal part of the trinity?

GOD CONSCIOUS OR SIN CONSCIOUS

Many believers have been taught that Holy Spirit has primarily come to convict us of our sin. With the myriad of operations that Holy Spirit performs, it's unfortunate that we tend to focus on this singular aspect of him.

I believe as we carefully look at the teaching of John 16, we will come to a different conclusion.

Jesus said:

> "Nevertheless I tell you the truth. It is to your advantage that I go away; for if I do not go away, the Helper will not come to you; but if I depart, I will send Him to you. And when He has come, He will convict the world of sin, and of righteousness, and of judgement: of sin, because they do not believe in Me; of righteousness, because I go to My Father and you see Me no more; of judgment, because the ruler of this world is judged."
> John 16:7-11

Notice the pronouns Jesus used to identify Holy Spirit's activity. He will convict the world of sin because they do not believe in me. He is addressing unbelievers, and unbelief is their sin.

Next, Jesus says Holy Spirit will convict some of righteousness "because I go to my Father, and you see me no more." Jesus is speaking to believers! Holy Spirit convicts or convinces believers of their righteousness.

Lastly, Holy Spirit convicts of Judgement because the ruler of this world is judged. This is important because Jesus is referring to the devil who is already judged and stripped of all authority.

This is so amazing! Holy Spirit comes to comfort us and convince us that we are not condemned. He is not a sin hunter, tracking down believers to convict us of our sin. He is with us to convince us that, because we are in Christ, we are righteous, loved, accepted, and forgiven.

THE HELPER

The Holy Spirit is called the Helper, and he is great at what he does. He knows the what, when, and how to lead us and keep us in alignment with God's plan for our lives.

When I was eighteen years old, I went off to Bible college and arrived several weeks early so I could find a job. Getting a job was a necessity for me to go to school so I was praying for God to open a door of opportunity.

I searched for a job for a week and I was coming up empty. It didn't help that the college was in a relatively small town and jobs were not typically easy to find there. At the same time, I was missing my fiancé who was 1,200 miles from where I was going to school.

I informed the Lord that if I didn't get a job, I would have to go home. At that moment, this option had some appeal.

Feeling somewhat desperate, I decided to pray a very challenging prayer. I got on my knees and said, "Lord, I am not getting off my knees until you let me know what to do."

Almost immediately, I remember thinking that this prayer might not have been the best way to go about it! I might be kneeling here for a long time.

He had compassion on my knees and within minutes, I heard Holy Spirit speak clearly: "Go to Ellendale Grain and Seed."

I graciously reminded the Lord that I had already been there and they told me there was no job available. I waited briefly and heard it again a second time: "Go to Ellendale Grain and Seed."

Hearing that, I smiled and said "Okay, Lord, I'll go…"

As I stood up, I heard the still small voice of Holy Spirit say, "Put on your work clothes." Now I was almost laughing. "They are going to think that I'm ridiculous."

I put on my bib overalls and drove my orange MGB roadster to Ellendale Grain and Seed.

I walked up to the office and no sooner had I walked inside the door that the man behind the counter said, "Are you the man we're looking for?" I said "Yes, I am!"

There was another young man in the office and they told us the truck was ready to take the two of us out to the field. Because I had my work clothes on, we were ready to go and buck hay in the fields.

The manager had called the college to send two students. I'm not sure what happened to the other guy, but I had a job at Ellendale Grain and Seed for my entire school year.

HOLY SPIRIT, YOUR ADVANTAGE

One of the many reasons Holy Spirit is so helpful is because he knows everything about everything. He is omniscient, or, all knowing, and he loves to share with us.

Jesus gave us some significant keys in his Word to help us understand the advantages of having his Holy Spirit.

> "Nevertheless I tell you the truth. It is to your advantage
> that I go away; for the Helper will not come to you; but
> if I depart, I will send Him to you."
> John 16:7

It's intriguing that the main focus of the Old Testament was God. Then, for thirty-three years, the focus shifted to Jesus as he fulfilled his ministry and made atonement through his finished work on the cross. After Jesus ascended, he sent the Holy Spirit to be the Triune God's representative on the Earth. Jesus left in order for the Holy Spirit to come.

Jesus said it would be to our advantage that he go away, and it's true. While Jesus could only be at one place at a time, Holy Spirit is able to indwell all believers, everywhere around the world, all at the same time. What a stellar Kingdom move! With the sending of Holy Spirit, every believer can now be filled with the awesome presence and power of Almighty God.

Can you imagine the nightmare when the devil discovered that all believers would now have authority over him and his demonic hordes? We must take advantage of our advantage by being filled with the Holy Spirit and exercise our authority over the Kingdom of Darkness!

Jesus said he would send the Holy Spirit, and that is why 120 believers were praying and waiting in the upper room.

> And being assembled together with them, He commanded them not to depart from Jerusalem, but to wait for the Promise of the Father, "which," He said, "you have heard from Me; for John truly baptized with water, but you shall be baptized with the Holy Spirit not many days from now."
> Acts 1:4-5

POWER ENCOUNTER

Jesus told his followers:

> "But you shall receive power when the Holy Spirit has come upon you; and you shall be witnesses to Me in Jerusalem, and in all Judea and Samaria, and to the end of the earth."
> Acts 1:8

This is the reason they were in the upper room. They were waiting for this powerful baptism in the Holy Spirit! They were promised that they would receive power when the Spirit came upon them. The Greek word for power here is "dunamis" which means miracle-working power. That word "dunamis" is the word from which we derive our English word, dynamite.

In 1867, Alfred Nobel discovered how to stabilize nitroglycerin and created gunpowder. The invention of dynamite marked a pivotal time of change in global industrialization. Dynamite made it easier to safely extract raw materials, allowing for more innovations to come to life. From mining to building roads, the power of dynamite brought exponential progress for building our modern society.

In much the same way, the demonstration of God's power brought great and impacting changes to building up and expanding the Kingdom of God to move forward. Signs, wonders, miracles, and healings powerfully paved the way for the growing fellowship. People believed because of the authority of the Word they spoke and the miracles they performed.

The supernatural manifestations became the trademark for the thriving fellowship.

In the last words Jesus spoke while on earth, he declared that his disciples would be witnesses to him in Jerusalem, Judea, Samaria, and to the ends of the earth. Then something wonderful and gloriously supernatural happened on the Day of Pentecost.

GOD'S GREAT SHOCK AND AWE

When the Day of Pentecost had fully come, they were all with one accord in one place. And suddenly there came a sound from heaven, as of a rushing mighty wind, and it filled the whole house where they were sitting.
Then there appeared to them divided tongues, as of fire, and one sat upon each of them. And they were all filled with the Holy Spirit and began to speak with other tongues, as the Spirit gave them utterance.
Acts 2:1-4

Those waiting in the upper room were in one accord, which means they were united in their identity, purpose, and passion. Unity attracts the presence of God, which we can see unfold right here in this powerful encounter.

There are a few details used to describe how Holy Spirit showed up that are important for us to pay close attention to.

They heard the sound of a rushing mighty wind. The Holy Spirit was represented by the sound of a rushing mighty wind. "Mighty wind" would better be translated as a violent wind. Imagine a hurricane-like sound! The Hebrew word for "Spirit" is Ruach, which refers to God as a breath, or wind. The Greek word used for "wind" means breath of life. This mighty wind appears to be God's way of showing how powerful the outpouring of his Spirit really is.

A flame of fire sat upon each one of them individually. I want to draw your attention to three Old Testament requirements that had to be in place in order for God's presence to dwell somewhere: there had to be a temple, a priest, and a sacrifice. When the tabernacle and temple were dedicated to God, the measurements and materials had to be exactly as God had prescribed them to Moses. When everything for the temple was complete and the people prayed, and it was the fire of God falling from Heaven and consuming the sacrifice that God used to say, "Yes, this is an acceptable place for me to inhabit."

The Holy Spirit flames of fire that fell upon the 120 believers on the Day of Pentecost communicated a major shift. The fire testified that God would now be dwelling within his people instead of inhabiting a man-made temple of stone.

The tongues and languages they each began to speak in. The word "language" here is the Greek word "dialektos" which is where we get the word dialect. Not only were the believers speaking in different languages but they were using the same dialect, idioms, phrases, and regional accents specific to each geographical location from which the listeners had come.

And there were dwelling in Jerusalem Jews, devout men, from every nation under heaven. And when this sound occurred, the multitude came together, and were confused, because everyone heard them speak in his own language. Then they were all amazed and marveled, saying to one another, "Look, are not all these who speak Galileans? And how is it that we hear, each in our own

language in which we were born?"
Acts 2:5-8

There were only 120 believers speaking in tongues, and there was a massive crowd of people listening in. That means this small group of 120 believers must have been speaking in a large variety of different dialects. This would have been amazing, even for a group of highly-educated language specialists! For a group of uneducated Galileans, it would simply be unheard of. It was a supernatural sign!

The Jewish pilgrims said to one another, "What could this mean?" The sign pointed them to the truth of Jesus' death, his resurrection, and his glorious exaltation at the right hand of the Father. It was this great segway that led up to Peter's powerful proclamation of the gospel and as a result, 3,000 people were born again and baptized that day.

The power unleashed through speaking in tongues is evident throughout the book of Acts and is still in operation today.

GOD'S NEW DWELLING PLACE

We are now God's chosen place to dwell. It's no coincidence that, as New Covenant believers, we are described in scripture as a temple, a priest, and a sacrifice.

1. Our body is called the TEMPLE of the Holy Spirit. (1 Corinthians 6:19)

2. We are called a royal PRIEST to our God. (1 Peter 2:9)

3. We are to present our bodies to God as a LIVING SACRIFICE. (Romans 12:1)

It's marvelous to know that we as believers are inhabited by the Spirit of Almighty God. Jesus let his disciples know that it was to their advantage that the Holy Spirit was coming. Likewise, it is incumbent upon us to take advantage of the powerful Holy Spirit dwelling within us.

NINE

FOLLOW THE LEADER

"The Holy Spirit is not 'the Doer,' but rather the 'Helper.' He will not do it without us, but if we engage, He will help us with what we need to make it happen."
- Rick Joyner

While seated in the Minneapolis Airport waiting for my flight to Boise, Idaho, the hours seemed to fly by. I was reading the fascinating book, *How to Live Like a King's Kid*, written by Harold Hill. It had me on the edge of my seat!

Harold's daily life was filled with supernatural experiences initiated by the Holy Spirit. These inspired Holy Spirit promptings opened doors of opportunity for him to minister to total strangers in seemingly random ways. He found himself in the right place, at the right time, with the right people, sharing simple truths with profound power. The results of his obedient actions were salvations, healings, and people being set free from bondage and addictions. Abundant life was being imparted!

While significantly inspired by his life story, I sensed another emotion surfacing. This emotion seemed to morph in intensity as I continued reading about the copious miracles, signs, and wonders Harold witnessed. Suddenly, I recognized that it was jealousy. I was jealous of how skillfully, powerfully, and seemingly effortlessly God had used Harold Hill to minister to people.

Perhaps being an eighteen-year-old freshman in Bible college was amplifying my FOMO (fear of missing out). As I laid the book on my lap, the unforgettable question I quietly asked was, "Lord, why don't you use me like you do Harold Hill?"

I distinctly heard an inner voice say, "Turn around and tell that man Jesus loves him."

I had been so inundated by my book that I hadn't realized there was a man standing behind me. He looked to be about forty years old. He was wearing a blue suit with an off-centered tie and had a look of deep anguish clouding his countenance as he drank hard liquor from a bottle.

Immediately, I drew from my vast reservoir of Bible college training in personal evangelism. I knew I needed to establish common ground with him before sharing Christ (the term "common ground" means finding areas of agreement or common interests).

I walked around the seats between us and began peppering him with common-ground questions. I discovered that he had lost his job and his family was in severe turmoil. He was reluctant to answer any more of my probing questions and after a couple more minutes, he stood up without another word and walked away.

How do you like that? I was there, poised to give him fervent evangelistic instructions with all the answers he needed, and he just walked away.

I felt disappointed and rejected as I returned to my seat. I picked up my book and before I could read a sentence, the Holy Spirit clearly spoke, "That's why I don't use you like I do Harold Hill. I told you to turn around and tell that man that Jesus loves him, but you had a better idea."

Ouch! I repented right away for ignoring the direct instructions from Holy Spirit. I made a heartfelt decision not to second guess the leading of the Holy Spirit again. I'm convinced that if I would have followed his simple divine instructions to tell that man that Jesus loves him, he would have encountered the life-altering power of Holy Spirit.

The epiphany that hit home for me was that God is more pleased with my obedience than my ministerial competence. When my trust is in the Lord and his wisdom, I can expect to experience abundant supernatural results.

While it's important for us to prepare and to understand principles that will assist us in reaching people for Christ, dependence and obedience to the Holy Spirit is priority number one.

PAUL'S PATTERN OF BEING LED

The Apostle Paul traveled extensively throughout the Roman Empire aggressively pursuing every opportunity to spread the good news of Jesus.

In studying the life and missionary work of the Apostle Paul, it is interesting to note that Paul did not learn a foreign language to do his missionary work. He used the Greek language, which he already spoke. He also used the Aramaic on occasion, perhaps Latin. These were also languages he already knew. Paul didn't travel to a foreign land to be a missionary, except for his time alone in the Arabian Desert. He was born in, lived in, and died, in the confines of the Roman Empire.

Even though he never left the Roman Empire, Paul was extremely proactive in his approach to evangelism. He would step out and pursue available opportunities, confident that God would ultimately lead him.

Paul embraced the understanding that motion often brings clarity, which is helpful to remember whenever we feel stuck. It's easier to steer a car when it's moving, and this appears to be the case for Paul in the book of Acts.

Paul and Silas traveled through the area of Phrygia and Galatia because the Holy Spirit had prevented them from preaching in Asia at that time. They headed north for the province of Bithynia, but again, the Spirit of Jesus did not allow them to go there.

Instead, they went on through Mysia to the seaport of Troas where Paul had a vision. In his vision, a man from Macedonia in northern Greece was standing there pleading with him, "Come over to Macedonia and help us!"

Paul and Silas left for Macedonia at once, having concluded that God was calling them to preach the Good News there. (Acts 16:9-10 NLT)

Have you ever wondered why God doesn't just hand us a playbook that includes all the things he wants us to do? It seems that it would be helpful to know the why, the when, the where, and the how in advance, doesn't it?

Perhaps it would be helpful for us to remember that two thirds of God's name is "Go." God designed us to walk by faith and be led by Holy Spirit and work with him as a team! Every effective team has a leader. Holy Spirit is our leader.

Have you noticed that God rarely operates in the timing and in the way that we think he will? For this reason, it's essential to trust and receive guidance from Holy Spirit, the one who knows everything about everything.

Not knowing the details of how, when, and where God is going to direct us keeps us in a mode of dependency upon him. I love the way Luke describes the partnership with the Holy Spirit while they were navigating their way through an extremely controversial decision. He said, "It seemed good to the Holy Spirit and to us..."

Following the breadcrumbs is a fitting description for how the Lord often leads us.

A SPIRIT-LED SHIFT

I met an apostle named Ron Johnson through a network of mutual friends. He pastored a large church on the East Coast and had come to speak at a few of our special services.

I picked Ron up at the hotel in the morning after his first night in Juneau. We had not spoken since he arrived late the night before. Once in my truck, his first words to me were, "Mike, God woke me up at 3 a.m. to tell me that your wife is going to tell you something, and you are supposed to listen to her."

He didn't know anything about our church and he didn't know my wife, Deenie. I thought it might be best for me not to share that word with Deenie right away.

Before our main Sunday service, Ron was training about thirty-five of our church leaders. As usual, Deenie and I were sitting in the front row. Deenie had her yellow notebook resting on her lap, pen in hand.

Suddenly, Deenie opened her notebook and started rapidly writing bullet points. She started elbowing me and loudly whispering, "Mike, Mike...Look at this."

Whispering as quietly as possible, I said, "Deenie, just wait." We were on the front row and I didn't want to distract everyone behind us.

"No, look at this!" She insisted.

A bit stressed, I looked over and whispered "What?"

Deenie pointed to the top bullet point and said, "We're supposed to do this!"

Her notes said, "Close Juneau Christian School."

"We don't have to do that!" I emphatically whispered.

Our school had been in operation for thirty years! It was the largest Christian school in our city and was highly regarded.

At that moment, I had totally forgotten the instructions from Ron.

The plot thickens!

Our son, Ben, and his wife, Heather, were the youth pastors of our church at the time. We had an intense desire to have a youth center for the youth of the church and our city. In fact, we had been looking all over the city for a facility to house a youth center.

Ben had been out of town speaking at a youth event in Wasilla, Alaska over this particular weekend, which is over 500 miles from Juneau. He called me Saturday night before our special meetings.

"Dad," he said, "God has downloaded something to me and I have to tell you!"

I said, "Then tell me."

He said, "No Dad, I need to tell you in person. I'm flying in on Sunday morning so I can tell you before the service."

So, Sunday morning after our class, Deenie, Ron and I were talking about the word she had just received in the leadership class. Right then, Ben came into my office fresh off his flight and shared with all of us what had been revealed to him the day before.

While he had been thinking about the youth center, Holy Spirit had communicated to him that the youth center was "in his hip pocket." He was puzzled at first, then received a literal vision of a beautiful, state-of-the-art youth center that was to be in our building. He said that Juneau Christian School was supposed to close.

RECALIBRATION OF VISION

While all of this was unfolding, I realized that we had been maintaining another man's vision for the past seventeen years. Juneau Christian School had been the vision of a former Pastor, George McNeven's. Holy Spirit was clearly revealing to us that we were supposed to transition our focus on our youth.

At that time, we were in the midst of a capital campaign to raise finances for a new sanctuary. We felt led by God to pivot our support, focus, energy, and finances to the new youth center rather than building a new sanctuary. Our church family was united in support of the new direction and we renovated 19,000 square feet of our facility to minister to youth, in what is now called the Hub Youth Center.

There were some in our community who were not pleased with us closing the school. Doing the will of God required us to face and overcome the fear of man.

Fearing people is a dangerous trap, but trusting the Lord means safety.
Proverbs 29:25 NLT

We finished out the school year before the school was moved to another church in Juneau. The new school year started on time, with a new name and identity, and has done very well for the past seventeen years.

Meanwhile, the Hub Youth Center has been a great blessing to our community and was made possible because, as a church family, we were willing to listen and come into alignment with the Holy Spirit as our leader.

Have you found yourself stressed out in the midst of seemingly unfavorable circumstances, not knowing what to do? What an excellent opportunity to seek the Lord and listen for instruction and direction from the Holy Spirit! It's awesome to receive prophetic words that are tailormade for your life.

TEN

STOLEN TREASURES

"The doctrine stating signs and wonders are no longer needed because we have the Bible was created by people who hadn't seen God's power and needed an explanation to justify their own powerless churches."
- Bill Johnson

Sherlock Holmes and his assistant, Watson, went camping in the desert. They set up their tent, then fell asleep. Some hours later, Sherlock woke his faithful friend.

"Watson, look up at the sky and tell me what you see," he said.

Watson replied, "I see millions of stars."

"What does that tell you?" Sherlock asked.

Watson pondered for a moment, then answered Sherlock's question by saying, "Astronomically, it tells me that Saturn is in Leo. Time wise, it appears to be approximately a quarter past three. Theologically, it's evident the Creator is all-powerful and we are small and insignificant in comparison. Meteorologically, it seems we will have a beautiful day tomorrow."

Watson asked in return, "What does it tell you, Sherlock?"

Sherlock was silent for a moment before answering, "Watson, it tells me someone has stolen our tent."

While Watson's observations regarding astronomy, time, theology and meteorology were commendable, he missed the obvious: their tent had been stolen. Right under their noses, they had lost their cover and protection from the elements.

I believe there is a parallel with this story and the tangled cessationism teachings. The term "cessationism" refers to the teaching that all the miraculous gifts practiced by the early church have been suspended for the duration of the present age. This doctrine teaches that spiritual gifts, such as speaking in tongues, prophecy, and healing, ceased with the death of the last apostle appointed by Jesus.

THE MAIN THING

Jesus said, "I will build my church and the gates of Hell shall not prevail against it." Jesus used the Greek word "Ecclesia" for church. Ecclesia was not a religious term; in fact, it was used to describe a gathering of people for any purpose. Jesus was telling his disciples that he would build up his people and that, through them, he would demonstrate triumphant victory over hell and the powers of darkness.

Jesus informed them of their main purpose:

Jesus came and told his disciples, "I have been given all authority in heaven and on earth. Therefore, go and make disciples of all the nations, baptizing them in the name of the Father and the Son and the Holy Spirit. Teach these new disciples to obey all the commands I have given you. And be sure of this: I am with you always, even to the end of the age."

Matthew 28:18-20 NLT

Earlier, Jesus had made it clear to his disciples that they were not to go until they had received what he was sending. Jesus was very emphatic when he told his disciples:

"Behold, I send the Promise of My Father upon you; but tarry in the city of Jerusalem until you are endued with power from on high."
Luke 24:49

The early church was born in power on the day of Pentecost, and through supernatural manifestations witnessed that day, the Jewish pilgrims from many nations asked the question, "What do these things mean?"

Peter gladly pontificated:

"But this is what which was spoken by the prophet Joel: 'And it shall come to pass in the last days, says God, that I will pour out of My Spirit on all flesh; your sons and your daughters shall prophesy, your young men shall see visions, your old men shall dream dreams. And on My menservants and on My maidservants I will pour out My Spirit in those days; And they shall prophesy."
Acts 2:16-18

After Peter preached, the people asked him, "What shall we do?" to which he replied:

"Repent, and let every one of you be baptized in the name of Jesus Christ for the remission of sins; and you shall receive the gift of the Holy Spirit. For the promise is to you and to your children, and to all who are afar off, as many as the Lord our God will call."
Acts 2:36-39

The strong emphasis on salvation, followed by the baptism in the Holy Spirit, continued to move powerfully within the church through messages like Peter's. Through the use of supernatural gifts of the Holy Spirit, the number of believers grew exponentially.

This was the beginning of the last days, and we are still living in the last days. There are still outpourings of the Holy Spirit all around the world, accompanied by supernatural manifestations and gifts. This dynamic outpouring described by the prophet Joel has and will continue to supernaturally impact the young and old, male and female, servants and handmaidens, and they will prophesy.

Much of the church has been cheated out of the supernatural inheritance that was meant for all believers to walk in. God never intended the church to lose the power and miracles the early church experienced.

HOLY HUNGER

It was a tiny, crude, wood building. Inside, four women were sitting in a short row of chairs while other women prayed passionately over them. I was only five years old, but I vividly remember watching these four women crying as the Holy Spirit moved upon their hearts. My mother was one of them.

This prayer event had not been scheduled by our church. This was a secret meeting scheduled for my mom and her friends to be baptized in the Holy Spirit.

You see, the church we attended believed that supernatural manifestations had ceased with the last apostle. When our pastor began hearing that people were receiving the baptism of the Holy Spirit, he began sending deacons to their homes to notify them that they were no longer welcome in our church. As a young child, I was puzzled.

Today, I'm proud of my mom and her friends for being willing to risk being shunned and ostracized from the church in order to receive everything God had for them.

MIRACLE-WORKING GOD

Albert Einstein said, "There are only two ways to live your life. One is as though nothing is a miracle. The other is as though everything is."

Our God is supernatural. We live on a planet that was spoken into existence without any preexisting material. It is spinning at 1,000 miles per hour while speeding through space at 66,000 miles per hour. It's miraculous that we are not perpetually dizzy and we can keep our balance!

On a day when you feel like you've been spinning your wheels without getting anywhere, take comfort in the fact that you did travel 1.6 million miles through space and stayed on schedule for our annual trip of 584 million miles around the sun.

We are enriched with incredible bodies. Without any conscious effort, we each take about 23,000 breaths a day. The average heart will beat 100,000 times today, circulating five quarts of blood through 100,000 miles of arteries, veins, and capillaries.

Let's face it, we experience God's miracle-working power every day. We have a miracle-working God who created us in his image, after his likeness, for his pleasure.

HEALING — IN THE ATONEMENT

While in Bible College, I started devouring books on healing. I recognized right away that "healing" included healing of every kind, including physical healings. All healing is included in the atonement that Jesus purchased on Calvary's cross.

Isaiah prophesied about the coming atonement:

But He was wounded for our transgressions, He was bruised for our iniquities; The chastisement for our peace was upon Him, And by His stripes we are healed.
Isaiah 53:5

Peter declared, "...who Himself bore our sins in His own body on the tree, that we, having died to sins, might live for righteousness— by whose stripes you were healed." (1 Peter 2:24)

Isaiah, looking forward to the cross, said, "by His stripes we are healed." Peter, looking back to the cross said, "...by whose stripes you were healed." Your healing has been secured for you through Jesus. We are to believe and receive it in Jesus' name.

CURSE CANCER

During that season of studying healing, my parents called me and I immediately detected sadness in their voices.

"Mike, it's about Kelly...."

My little sister, Kelly, has always been very goal-oriented and extremely bright. She was a straight-A student from grade school through medical school. Little Miss 4.0 (a little annoying right?). Actually, I've always been very proud of her accomplishments.

As a young teen, she became a hospital volunteer, also known as a "candy striper." She worked without pay in a variety of healthcare settings under the direct supervision of nurses. At that time in my life, I didn't see the benefit of going to work and not receiving a paycheck. Now I realize Kelly's life goals and aspirations were spot on.

When Kelly was fourteen years old, Kelly had a mole removed from under her eyebrow which surprisingly turned out to be cancer. She received extensive surgery to clear the cancer.

Five years later, when Kelly was in college she noticed a growth appearing in exactly the same place above her eye where she had the cancer surgery.

On the phone call, my parents briefed me on the news that the growth had come back and this time, it was worse.

When I asked to speak with Kelly, her voice was filled with fear and sadness. In that moment, Holy Spirit told me exactly to say:

"Kelly, this is an attack of Satan against you and I curse that cancer in Jesus' name."

As I spoke those words, I felt a strong surge of faith, power, and confidence was activated and Kelly was blessed, encouraged, and relieved.

Three days later, the cancerous growth fell from above her eye onto her pillow. I'm convinced that the cancer died at the root when it was cursed, and in three days it dried up, fell off, and never came back.

Twelve-hundred miles separated us, but through the spoken word, Kelly received her complete healing and deliverance from cancer. Holy Spirit had prepared me to respond in faith the moment my sister needed it through his Word, prayer, and the healing testimonies I'd been reading.

I know very well that many pontificate that the day of miracles, signs, wonders, and gifts of the Holy Spirit are over. But, they are too late for those of us who are presently experiencing His powerful life-transforming results.

IT'S SUPERNATURAL

Our desire to see God move powerfully in our lives causes us to be aware and available for moments like this one where God can use us.

Those who believe the teachings of cessationists are unlikely candidates for experiencing faith activations like the one I had with my sister. How disappointing that would be! How many Christians have become impervious to receiving their full healing due to the persuasion that the time of signs, wonders, and miracles are over?

Even Jesus was impacted by the unbelief of people in his own hometown.

Now He could do no mighty work there, except that He

laid His hands on a few sick people and healed them.
And He marveled because of their unbelief....
Mark 6:5-6

Fortunately, the person who desires to experience God's
supernatural power is not at the mercy of those who merely have a
different opinion about the subject. When we have faith that signs,
wonders, and miracles are still in effect, we make ourselves available
to operate in the supernatural giftings of God and flow with power,
just like the believers in the book of Acts.

Jesus insisted that his disciples wait for the promise of the
baptism in the Holy Spirit, even though they had already partnered
in ministry with him for three years. Before the outpouring of
Pentecost, the resurrected Jesus said to them:

"Peace to you! As the Father has sent Me, I also send
you." And when He had said this, He breathed on them,
and said to them, "Receive the Holy Spirit."
John 20:21-22

His disciples received the gift of the Holy Spirit from Jesus right
then. However, this was different from the immersion of the Holy
Spirit they later experienced on the Day of Pentecost.

You see, all born-again believers have the Holy Spirit within
them. However, the book of Acts presents another invitation for
believers to also receive baptism in the Holy Spirit.

The Jews were surprised when the Gentiles received the baptism
in the Holy Spirit because they were not even expecting salvation to
be extended to them.

The Jewish believers who came with Peter were amazed
that the gift of the Holy Spirit had been poured out on
the Gentiles, too. For they heard them speaking in other
tongues and praising God.

Acts10:45-46 NLT

The Apostle Paul wrote about the importance of speaking in "other tongues" and he practiced what he preached. He said, "I thank my God I speak with tongues more than you all…" (1 Corinthians 14:18).

EMBRACING GOD'S SUPERNATURAL POWER

We live in a world where many people believe in supernatural power apart from God and his Word.

Those who engage in the occult and other forms of witchcraft can indeed encounter a supernatural force. However, this dark force will not produce light or life. Rather, the power of the enemy opens doors of demonic oppression, which leads to bondage and deception.

Some back away from Holy Spirit's power because the enemy can demonstrate powers of darkness. Others avoid the Holy Spirit because they have heard talk regarding some who misused the gifts of the Holy Spirit.

This line of reasoning is similar to someone who refuses to drive their car again because they know someone who drove recklessly, crashed, and was killed. We know that in the midst of thousands of safe drivers, there will always be some on the road who should abstain from driving.

Jesus said that false prophets would rise up and deceive many (Matthew 24:11). The fact that there are many false prophets doesn't negate the legitimate prophets. Actually, it adds support to the fact that there are true prophets of God because Satan will always counterfeit the real deal.

The point is, the enemy will endeavor to sidetrack and derail people from the purposes of God by pointing out those who are false or in error.

To quote the Sherlock Holmes' revelation: "Watson, someone

has stolen our tent." Many are being ripped off by distraction and are seemingly blinded to all that they have lost.

It is a travesty that so many have forfeited their spiritual inheritance. They miss being fully equipped for the main event because they have focussed on the wrong things.

I've heard some ask, "How do you know the power and the gifts you flow in are of God?"

That's not a problem because Holy Spirit, the third member of the trinity, promises to give us discernment and lead us into all truth.

It amazes me that so many Christians have more confidence in the devil's power to deceive than God's power to give us discernment and lead us into all truth. So many Christians are afraid of the Holy Spirit's awesome manifestations. When you want to identify a tree, take a look at its fruit.

The spirit of fear must not have any place in our heart or mind. The Apostle Paul told Timothy, "God has not given us a spirit of fear, but of love and power and of a sound mind." (2 Timothy 1:7)

DIVINE HEALING — FOR TODAY

We need to study the life of Jesus and the amazing example of his ministry. God anointed Jesus with the Holy Spirit, who then went about doing good and healing all who were oppressed of the devil (Acts 10:38).

Many people have been taught that God places sickness on us in order to teach us important lessons. As a mom or dad, would you place sickness on your children in order to teach them to be a better listener? Would you say, "Hey little buddy, if you don't stop crying, I'm going to have to slam the door on your fingers again. Daddy just wants to make sure you learn the important lessons he's teaching you."

The teaching that God afflicts us with sickness is twisted and tangled. Too many Christians choose the wisdom of man over the

Word of God.

Jesus is the image of God and his actions demonstrate the will of God for our lives. Jesus' will is to do good, heal, and deliver those who are oppressed of the devil. We need to take authority over the enemy because we have authority over oppression and all the works of the devil. This includes sickness.

UNWELCOME INTRUDER EXPOSED

Many years ago, I came home after work and when I stepped into our dining room, I felt something odd. As I looked to my left, I saw a shadowy being which I instantly knew was a demon.

When the demon recognized that I had seen it, it began cowering backward with its hands up around its face. I took a couple of steps and loudly said, "Get out of here in Jesus' name!" I'm not even sure that I needed to say that because it left quickly.

Right after that incident, I asked the Lord why he allowed me to see that demon. He shared with me that it was a spirit of infirmity.

I went into our bedroom and my wife, Deenie, was in bed because she had suddenly become very sick. I prayed and spoke healing over her body, and the sickness was gone almost immediately.

I'm sharing this story because we are in a spiritual battle and, like it or not, we don't have the option to go A.W.O.L. The enemy often goes unseen and undetected, using the invisible nature of the spiritual realm to try to ambush us in warfare. We must engage our faith, being filled with and led by the Holy Spirit, to detect and defeat every attack brought against us.

So then, surrender to God. Stand up to the devil and resist him. and he will flee in agony.
James 4:7 TPT

Jesus said:

"Most assuredly, I say to you, he who believes in Me, the works that I do he will do also; and greater works than these he will do, because I go to My Father."
John 14:12

GO WITH THE GOODS — STAY WITH THE STUFF

Jesus is a healer, deliverer, and savior! That means he can use us to do these things, too!

The Apostle Paul didn't back away from the supernatural power of God, but showed that it is an essential ingredient of the good news.

For I am not ashamed of the gospel of Christ, for it is the power of God to salvation for everyone who believes…
Romans 1:16a

The word "salvation" in the above scripture is the Greek word "soteria" from sozo, which includes: welfare, prosperity, deliverance, preservation, salvation, and safety.

Many Christians have settled for a belief in Jesus which doesn't include the power and authority of Jesus operating within their lives.

Apostle Paul became persuaded through his own personal encounter with Jesus that there is far more to sharing the good news than teaching people about God. He knew they needed to encounter Jesus' power for themselves:

So I have reason to be enthusiastic about all Christ Jesus has done through me in my service to God. Yet I dare not boast about anything except what Christ has done through me, bringing the Gentiles to God by my

message and by the way I worked among them. They were convinced by the power of miraculous signs and wonders and by the power of God's Spirit. In this way, I have fully presented the Good News of Christ from Jerusalem all the way to Illyricum.
Romans 15:17-19 NLT

And my speech and my preaching were not with persuasive words of human wisdom, but in demonstration of the Spirit and of power, that your faith should not be in the wisdom of men but in the power of God.
1 Corinthians 2:4-5

We are all called to function with the unction of Holy Spirit power. Remember: The main thing is to keep the main thing the main thing!

ELEVEN

SPIRIT DISCOVERY

"Having a renewed mind is often not an issue of whether or not someone is going to heaven, but of how much of heaven he or she wants in his or her life right now." - Bill Johnson

I t's essential that we understand that we are a spirit, we have a soul, and we live in a body.

Now may the God of peace Himself sanctify you completely; and may your whole spirit, soul, and body be preserved blameless at the coming of our Lord Jesus Christ. He who calls you is faithful, who also will do it. 1 Thessalonians 5:23

UNDERSTANDING SPIRIT SOUL AND BODY

Many Christians try to function on two of our three parts: the soul and the body. We all have a physical body which we can see and touch. We all have a soul: it's our mind, will, and emotions, or, our personality.

We deal with our body all the time. If I asked you how you feel, you would be able to give me an answer. We're also in touch with our emotions. We know if we are encouraged or discouraged, happy, angry, sad, or peaceful.

We are constantly monitoring our bodies and our souls, but most people don't recognize their spirit. Possibly that's because the spirit and soul are invisible, so we sense them interchangeably. However, this verse in Thessalonians lets us know that there are three distinct parts to us.

Our spirit is important because it's where our new identity in Christ operates within us from. Our spirits are as saved as they will ever be. Our souls, on the other hand, are not saved. When we're born again, it's our spirit that gets saved.

So, how do we discover our spirit when we can't feel it or see it? Jesus said: "That which is born of the flesh is flesh, that which is of the spirit is spirit." (John 3:6)

In this, Jesus was revealing to Nicodemus that spirit and flesh are in different realms.

If we want to know what is happening in our soul, we can pay attention to how we're feeling emotionally. If we want to see if there is anything on our teeth, we can look in the mirror.

WORD OF GOD - SPIRITUAL MIRROR

So, what about our spirit? James gives us a clue that the Word of God acts as a spiritual mirror:

For if anyone is a hearer of the word and not a doer, he is like a man observing his natural face in a mirror; for he observes himself, goes away, and immediately forgets what kind of man he was. But he who looks into the perfect law of liberty and continues in it, and is not a forgetful hearer but a doer of the work, this one will be blessed in what he does.

James 1:23-25

The Word of God is the perfect law of liberty and it is like a spiritual mirror.

When you look in a mirror, you're not actually seeing your face, you are seeing a reflection of your face. You have never really seen your face, but you can trust the image in your mirror to reflect back to you what you look like. You might comb your hair and put on makeup based on that reflection of yourself.

In that same way, we can trust the Word of God to reflect what our spirit looks like.

Our first understanding of our spirit is that it was dead. Let's go back to the beginning in the Garden of Eden.

DEATH TO LIFE

And the Lord God commanded the man, saying, "Of every tree of the garden you may freely eat; but of the tree of the knowledge of good and evil you shall not eat, for in the day that you eat of it you shall surely die."

Genesis 2:16-17

We know that Adam and Eve did not die physically the day they ate of the tree because they were expelled from the garden. We know that they did not die in their souls because they felt fear and shame as they hid from God. They died in their spirits.

That is where all of us since Adam have ended up, dead in our trespasses and sins. Thus in the garden after man sinned, we hear the sad words of separation from the Lord God calling out, "Adam where are you?"

This was not an insignificant issue. Adam and Eve rebelled against God's command. They actually chose to believe Satan's word above God's.

It's difficult for us to imagine how utterly horrible the collateral damage was for all mankind by this one decision.

> Therefore, just as through one man sin entered the world, and death through sin, and thus death spread to all men, because all sinned...
> Romans 5:12

I'm so thankful that God made a way for us to be delivered! Jesus is the way.

> ...For if by the one man's offense death reigned through the one, much more those who receive abundance of grace and of the gift of righteousness will reign in life through the One, Jesus Christ.
> Romans 5:17

> God made him who had no sin to be sin for us, so that in him we might become the righteousness of God.
> 2 Corinthians 5:21 NIV

> And you He made alive, who were dead in trespasses and sins...
> Ephesians 2:1

True Christianity is not about bad people becoming good people. It's about spiritually dead people being made spiritually alive through Christ because of God's great love for us!

Our spirit was dead, but God made us alive in Christ. He did something amazing in our born-again spirits. Your born-again spirit is righteous, pure, and holy.

UNDERSTANDING OUR SPIRIT IS THE KEY

The Apostle Paul said:

> This includes you who were once far away from God. You were his enemies, separated from him by your evil thoughts and actions. Yet now he has reconciled you to himself through the death of Christ in his physical body. As a result, he has brought you into his own presence, and you are holy and blameless as you stand before him without a single fault.
> Colossians 1:21-22 NLT

In our souls and bodies, we are not holy and blameless, but in our spirits, we are. We are looking through the mirror of the Word at our born-again spirits. When you and I believed in Jesus, we were sealed with the Holy Spirit.

The Apostle Paul said it this way:

> In Him you also trusted, after you heard the word of truth, the gospel of your salvation; in whom also, having believed, you were sealed with the Holy Spirit of promise, who is the guarantee of our inheritance until the redemption of the purchased possession, to the praise of His glory.
> Ephesians 1:13-14

When someone cans food, they seal the jars with paraffin, which makes an airtight seal that will protect and preserve the food within. This is how the word "seal" is used in this verse. When you were born again, your spirit was immediately vacuum packed by the Holy Spirit, keeping the good in and the bad out.

Your born-again spirit, or "new man," was created in righteousness and true holiness. Paul told us to put on the new man which was created according to God, in true righteousness and holiness (Ephesians 4:24b).

Your spirit became as Jesus is right here in this world. As he is, so are we in this world (I John 4:17 NKJV).

Let's examine another scripture through the mirror of the Word.

OLD THINGS HAVE PASSED AWAY

Therefore, if anyone is in Christ, he is a new creation; old things have passed away; behold, all things have become new.
2 Corinthians 5:17

This verse created a quandary for me because it says that the old things have passed away, not that they are gradually passing away.

After I was born again, I was very aware of some old things in my mindset and my will that had not yet passed away. I struggled to make sense of the "old things passed away, all things have become new" piece of this scripture. Since then, I've learned that from the vantage point of our born-again, sealed spirit, it makes perfect sense!

The mirror of scripture also tells us that our spirit became one with the Lord.

He that is joined to the Lord is one spirit.
1 Corinthians 6:7

Because we are joined to the Lord and we are one spirit, we are not limited by what we can know with our soul (mind, will, and emotions).

Consider the following verses:

> But you have an anointing from the Holy One, and you
> know all things.
> 1 John 2:20

On occasion, my wife has told me that I think I know everything, but I think she was being sarcastic.

> For "who has known the mind of the Lord that he may
> instruct Him?" But we have the mind of Christ.
> 1 Corinthians 2:16

Some people push back when we speak of the miraculous capabilities of our born-again spirit. This should not be hard to comprehend because our spirit has been birthed and sealed by the Holy Spirit.

BEHAVING LIKE ORDINARY PEOPLE

Many believers are uninformed of what God has already given to them and because of that, they find themselves living below their privileged position.

When we don't access the gifts God has already given us, we are unable to do all that God has planned for us to do.

The Apostle Paul challenged the Corinthian believers on their immature behavior:

> And I, brethren, could not speak to you as to spiritual
> people but as to carnal, as to babes in Christ. I fed you
> with milk and not with solid food; for until now you

were not able to receive it, and even now you are still not able; for you are still carnal. For where there are envy, strife, and divisions among you, are you not carnal and behaving like mere men?

1 Corinthians 3:1-3

Paul's expectations of the Corinthian believers reveal that we are not meant to behave like mere men and women.

Paul used the word "carnal" three times in the above passage of scripture.

In the Greek, this word is "sarkikos," meaning being led by the flesh; of the senses; being led by an unrenewed mind; being governed by human nature, instead of by the Spirit of God.

Paul was calling them up from being controlled by their senses and fleshly desires. He was unable to share deeper spiritual truth with them because they had chosen to be led by their flesh and human nature rather than the divine nature already within them.

In Philemon 1:6, Paul gives us a powerful key to activate what God has already given us when he writes, "that the sharing of your faith may become effective by the acknowledgment of every good thing which is in you in Christ Jesus."

FAITH IS ACTIVATED WHEN WE ENGAGE

Even though God has done great things through us and has a powerful future for us, it is up to us to activate his blessings in our lives. That's why Paul says, "That the sharing of your faith may become effective…"

The word "effective" is the Greek word "energeo." It is where we get the word energy. However, in this verse the word "energeo" carries the idea of something that has suddenly been energized or activated.

A car may be filled with enough gas to drive a long distance, but it won't go anywhere until someone puts the key into the ignition and turns the key or pushes the ignition button. The moment that key is turned, the combustion engine fires up. At that point, the engine has been activated and the potential of that car is unleashed.

The car always had the capability of moving, but if it is never activated, it sits dormant in the driveway. No matter how much fuel is in the tank or how much horsepower that car possesses, it's power and potential will never be realized until someone activates the ignition.

In Philemon 1:6, Paul writes about the acknowledgment of every good thing which is in you in Christ Jesus. Consider this: He saved you, healed you, redeemed you, and protected you. He has provided for you and continues to provide for you. He has given you a sound mind; the mind of Christ. He has imparted gifts and talents to you. He has planned a future for your life that is glorious. You are loaded with amazing potential that is just waiting to be activated!

Some believers feel that what the Word of God says about them and their own real-life experience doesn't line up. It seems like there is a big gap between what the Word of God says about them and how they feel and think about themselves.

This is a great example of experiencing life from our soul realm. Living life from our senses, our feelings, and our emotions will lead us to unbelief and fear. This is why Paul instructs us to not conform to this world, but to be transformed by the renewing of our minds. This is how we prove what the good, acceptable, and perfect will of God is.

Our minds need to be renewed by the Word of God to realize and release what God has already given us.

The Apostle Peter makes it clear that God has already given us everything we need through our relationship with Christ:

> By his divine power, God has given us everything we need for living a godly life. We have received all of this by coming to know him, the one who called us to

himself by means of his marvelous glory and excellence. And because of his glory and excellence, he has given us great and precious promises. These are the promises that enable you to share his divine nature and escape the world's corruption caused by human desires.

2 Peter 1:3-4 NLT

When you speak the Word of God in faith, you release the potential you possess in Jesus Christ and it is supernaturally ignited, activated, and released inside of you. The time spent in discovery with God and his Word is a rich investment in your life today and forever.

TWELVE

IDENTITY THEFT

"Royalty is my identity. Servanthood is my assignment.
Intimacy with God is my life source." - Bill Johnson

A FAMOUS THIEF

Arthur Barry gained an international reputation for being among the most outstanding jewel thieves of all time. Arthur Barry's "career" as a thief was unique in that his pursuit focused on high-class jewels and targeted rich people.

He managed his "job" very neatly without a single killing, injury, or bloodshed incident. He never stole cash and preferred to work in the presence of his (as he referred to them) "clients."

This fearless crusader didn't spare even the king's relatives, and wealthy tycoons were his specialty. Soon, his selective strikes on the rich became famous! Being robbed by this "gentlemen thief" became a status symbol among the elite and an embarrassment for the police and detectives. That is, until one night when Barry got caught during a robbery and was shot three times. With bullets in his body and splinters of glass in his eyes, he said, "I'm never going to do this again!"

He escaped arrest and hid out for three years before he was turned in by a jealous woman.

Barry served an eighteen-year prison sentence and when he was released, he kept his word, never returning to his life as a jewel thief. He came out of prison with the new identity as an upright citizen. As a matter of fact, he settled in a small New England town and began to live a model life where he was elected as the commander of the local Veterans organization.

Eventually, however, word leaked out in his New England town that the famous jewel thief was in their midst. Reporters from all over the country came to the little town to interview him.

One reporter got to the very crux of the matter when he asked the most penetrating question of all: "Mr. Barry, you stole from a lot of wealthy people during your years as a thief. I'm curious to know if you remember from whom you stole the most?"

Without hesitation, Barry said, "That's easy. The man from whom I stole the most was Arthur Barry. I could have been a successful businessman, a baron on Wall Street, and a contributing member to society. But instead I chose the life of a thief and spent two-thirds of my adult life behind prison bars."

CLEVER CROOKS

Unfortunately, there are many thieves in our society who specialize in taking other people's identities. There were 4.8 million identity theft and fraud reports received by the Federal Trade Commission in 2020, a 45 percent increase from the 3.3 million cases reported in 2019. There was a 113 percent increase in identity theft complaints.

Identity theft is the act of stealing a victim's Personal Identifying

Information (PII), which could include name, address, Social Security number, and other identifying numbers such as medical insurance or credit card accounts.

Phishing scammers often use emails to trick victims into providing personal or financial information.

During the writing of this book, I had two people that I know message me through Facebook. The conversation started with small talk, then they quickly asked me if I had heard the good news about the federal grant program. They both told me that they had received a $250,000 grant which doesn't have to be paid back!

It sounded too good to be true, and it was. When I called one of the individuals who supposedly sent the message, they had no idea that their identity had been hacked and used for an attempted scam against me.

Like identity thieves, the devil has been very successful at subverting and derailing many believers from knowing their true identity in Christ.

In the Garden of Eden, Lucifer was extremely cunning in convincing Eve that God was holding her back from the best life that the tree of knowledge of good and evil could give her. Somehow, she was distracted from her amazingly privileged high and holy identity as a daughter of Almighty God.

Knowing Eve's experience of God's goodness, Satan knew that she could not be lured away from God with evil. Instead, he cleverly camouflaged the poisonous produce as something good, gaining the advantage for the steal.

So when the woman saw that the tree was good for food, that it was pleasant to the eyes, and a tree desirable to make one wise, she took of its fruit and ate.
Genesis 3:6

It wasn't the evil side of the tree of the knowledge of good and evil that Eve was drawn to. It was the good side. The Bible describes it as good, pleasant to the eyes, and desirable to make one wise. What could be wrong with good, pleasant, and desirable?

It was good, but it was not from God. That can be very deceiving. There are many who have been deceived into believing that they don't need a savior because they are basically good people who do good things. That's when "good" becomes the enemy of "best."

HOW MANY RIGHTEOUS PEOPLE HERE?

Our identity affects our wholeness. We were born into a fallen world with a fallen identity. As a result, we often struggle with feelings of brokenness, inferiority, low self esteem, and confusion. When we question who we are in Christ, Satan is quick to help us feed on wrong answers.

Years ago, we had a guest teacher in our church who started out by asking the question: "How many righteous people do we have here this morning?" The question seemed to hang in the air, perplexing the Sunday morning congregation at Juneau Christian Center.

Only a few hands went up.

It wasn't a trick question; it was being used like a dipstick to measure the oil level of a car. Our guest speaker was probing to know the level of our understanding of our righteousness.

He looked at me and said, "I have my work cut out for me."

At that time, we did not understand our righteousness in Christ Jesus. We didn't understand that our good standing with Jesus wasn't at all based on our good works, but part of the great exchange made on the cross:

For He made Him who knew no sin to be sin for us, that we might become the righteousness of God in Him.
2 Corinthians 5:21

WE ARE GOD'S MASTERPIECE

The Apostle Paul said:

For we are God's masterpiece. He has created us anew
in Christ Jesus, so we can do the good things he planned
for us long ago.
Ephesians 2:10 NLT

I love that God has created us in Christ's image, which enables
us to live in victory, enjoy abundant life, and do those good things he
planned for us long ago. We are not an afterthought in the mind of
our generous, gracious God.

God obviously highly values us. His creativity is demonstrated
through the spectacularly intricate creation of our bodies. Every
human cell has around six feet of DNA. Our DNA code is really
the "language of life," containing the instructions for making a living
thing.

Let's say each human has around 10-trillion cells (this is a lowball
estimate). This would mean that each person has around 60-trillion
feet (around 10-billion miles) of DNA inside of them. Your DNA
can stretch to the moon and back 1,500 times and reach the sun and
back four times.

No one else has your fingerprint or your DNA. You are created
on purpose for a very unique purpose in God. Once we discover our
unique identity in Christ, it frees us to be who God created us to be.

We are created for a special purpose on purpose. Once we find
our true identity in Christ, we can make peace with our individuality.
We can be who God made us to be because he made us for a special
purpose.

God's purpose for birds is that they may fly, so he made them
with feathers and light bones. They can fly because their divine
design matches their divine purpose.

OUR DIVINE DESIGN

The divine design for our bodies is on display through pure brain science.

Dr. Caroline Leaf, author of the book *Switch On Your Brain* is a brilliant and prolific communicator, pathologist, and cognitive neuroscientist with over thirty years in research and study.

In her book, she said:

Breakthrough neuroscientific research is confirming daily what we instinctively knew all along: What you are thinking every moment of everyday becomes a physical reality in your brain and body, which affects your optimal mental and physical health.

These thoughts collectively form your attitude, which is your state of mind. It's your attitude, not your DNA, that determines so much of the quality of your life! This state of mind is real, physical, electromagnetic, quantum, and chemical flow in the brain that switches groups of genes on or off in a positive or negative direction based on your choices and subsequent reactions.

There are 1,400 chemical responses which negatively impact your body when you go into fear and irritation.

Dr. Caroline also said:

So in the human physical body, we do not have any subatomic particles or structures within our cells, or structures within our brain or body, or circuits, neurotransmitters, anything for negativity. So worry, fear, anxiety, irritation, frustration, lack of joy, lack of peace, hatred, all that toxic stuff, trauma, and bullying.We don't have anything for that, so those are created results of our thinking, and feeling, and choosing.

Dr. Leaf's research shows that we are made for love. We don't actually have circuitry for toxicity, negativity and fear. We are hardwired by our creator to love and live positive lives.When we don't love others well, our brains are literally clouded. Still, God allows us to choose how we will respond to the challenges of everyday life.

A DOWNLOAD FOR AN UPLIFT

Several years ago, I woke up early in the morning hearing several phrases in my mind I believed were from the Lord. I went into my office and began to write them down so I wouldn't lose this download:

"Faith, not fear; positive, not negative; hope, not despair; courage, not discouraged; strength, not weakness; built up, not torn down; fearless, not fretful; prayerful, not anxious; bold, not timid."

Soon after I received this, I went through a very difficult time in my life. It dawned on me that God had given me those phrases as a grid to help me identify my choices, and respond in faith rather than reacting in fear.

Each of these phrases gives us a choice of how we can respond to life's challenges. Our identity in Christ will always lead us toward our preferred response in faith, which is: positive, hope, courage, strength, built up, fearless, prayerful, and bold.

Our identity is connected to our purpose. Without purpose, we lose passion for life. Our identity connects us to our course in life. The devil tries to blind us from our true identity so that he can derail our purpose and thus, alter the trajectory of our life. But, we have the Greater One living on the inside of us, and greater is he that is in us than he that is in the world (1 John 4:4).

We don't get a dress rehearsal for our lives. We get one shot at it. Arthur Barry had years in jail to ponder his many "if onlys" while serving his sentence in confinement. Thankfully he turned his "if onlys" into "what ifs?"

Do you realize that no one can cap or sabotage your success on the path called life's destiny? With God's help, we can use the obstacles we face as a springboard to launch us into our God ordained destiny. Our "if onlys," "shoulda," "woulda," and "coulda"s need to be replaced with more positive questions, like: "what if?" -

What if you and I were to seek God to know our true, unique identity in Christ? What if we truly believed that we can do all things through Christ who strengthens us? What if we invested our lives in doing God's will? What if you and I consistently chose to seek first the Kingdom of God, and his righteousness? What If we trusted in the Lord with all of our heart and leaned not on our own understanding? What if we chose to make him the Lord of every part of our lives? What if we chose to believe that we have been made to be the righteousness of God in Christ Jesus?

WITH HIM WE ARE ENOUGH

Most of us have wrestled with thoughts that try to convince us that we are not enough. Not enough for our job; not enough for our family; not enough to accomplish what we hope to accomplish with our lives.

God has provided for us the complete package for abundant life in the here and now. The Apostle Paul explains our wonderful and miraculous relational position in Jesus Christ:

> For in Him dwells all the fullness of the Godhead bodily; and you are complete in Him, who is the head of all principality and power.
> Colossians 2:9-10

We are complete in him! Because of our union with Jesus, we have access to everything he has. Even though I have studied who I am in Christ for many years, I continue to be blown away at how awesome our born-again spirit is and how amazing our position in Christ is!

Did you know that God refers to us as sons and daughters, not as servants or slaves? We are heirs of God and joint heirs with Jesus Christ.

Jesus, the only begotten Son of God, is the natural "heir" of the Father. Christ's inheritance is the whole universe. It's all that is in existence.

Hebrews 1:2 says that the Son has been appointed heir of all things. Being a co-heir with Christ means that we, as God's adopted children, will share in the inheritance of Jesus.

What belongs to Jesus will also belong to us. Christ gives us his glory, his riches, and all things. We are as welcome in God's family as Jesus is! We are accepted by the beloved. As co-heirs, all that belongs to Jesus Christ will belong to us, as well.

Think of all that this means. Everything that God owns belongs to us, as well, because we belong to him. Our eternal inheritance as co-heirs with Christ is the result of the amazing grace of God.

When we have revelation of how much God loves us and how extravagant his mercy, grace, and favor are for us, we will live with confidence in our identity in Christ.

CREATOR KNOWS BEST

I love the story of Henry Ford and Charlie Steinmetz. Steinmetz, an engineering pioneer and legend, was an absolute genius in the field of electricity. Steinmetz stands with Thomas Edison and Elihu Thomas as the founding fathers of electricity. It's no wonder that Henry Ford hired Steinmetz to build the great generators that powered the enormous Ford plant.

Some time later, the generators broke down and Ford hired some local mechanics to fix the problem. They were unable to get the job done.

Ford was losing money, so he called Charlie to come and fix the generators. He came and tinkered on those generators for a couple of hours and threw the switch. The Ford plant was back in operation.

A couple of weeks later, Ford received the bill from Steinmetz for $10,000. Ford was a rich man, but he thought the amount that he had been charged was over the top. He wrote Steinmetz saying, "Charlie, isn't this a little much for a few hours of tinkering on those generators?"

Charlie itemized the bill and sent it back to Ford. The bill said, "For a few hours of tinkering: $10. For knowing where to tinker: $9,990." Henry Ford paid the bill.

Because Charlie had designed and created those generators, he was also the most capable person to repair and restore them for the purpose of generating power to the Ford Plant.

Charlie Steinmetz knew how incredibly gifted he was. He also seemed to understand how valuable his contribution was in moving America forward on its path to greater industrialization.

Almighty God, our designer, creator, and savior is the only one who is qualified to repair, restore, and empower our lives to live the abundant life through Jesus Christ.

May God supply the awesome revelation for us to know all that we are in Christ. May he also help us to access everything that has been given to us through him. May God be glorified through our lives in him!

NOTES

CHAPTER ONE

Genesis 2:8-9 (NKJV)
Acts 3:15
John 11:25
John 14:6
John 1:4
Genesis 2:16-17
Genesis 3:1
Genesis 3:2-3
Genesis 3:4-5
Genesis 1:37
1 Corinthians 15:56
2 Corinthians 3:7,9
Genesis 3:11b-12

To mortally wound or crush the head of Satan. To bruise the head is a picture of fatal and final destruction. To bruise the heel is a picture of damage, which is neither fatal nor final.

Genesis 3:14-15
John 12:31-32
Colossians 2:13-14
1 John 3:8
Romans 5:17-18

CHAPTER TWO

2 Timothy 2:15

Word study
Greek orthotomounta - #3718 means to make a straight cut, to dissect correctly.
Hebrew word - Bereeth - #1285 In the sense of cutting, passing between pieces of flesh.

New Strongs Exhaustive Concordance of Bible
James Strong, LL.,S.T.D.
Thomas Nelson Publishers. Copyright 1995

Genesis 12:1-3
Genesis 12:10-20
Genesis 26:1-16
Genesis 34
Genesis 38:11-26
Genesis 37:12-36
Exodus 15:22-16:35
Exodus 17:1-7

Chad Mansbridge *He Qualifies You* New Nature Publications, third edition 2013, Pg 19:

> Under the Abrahamic covenant; God's promises become your right and inheritance because of your pedigree.
> Under the Mosaic Law Covenant; God's promises are your right and inheritance, because of your performance.
> Under the New Covenant Agreement, through the Gospel of Jesus, God's promised blessings are your right and inheritance purely because of your position in Christ.

CHAPTER THREE

Leviticus 26:46
Exodus 19:3-17
Numbers 11
Numbers 12
1 Corinthians 15:56

The root of the Hebrew term used to refer to Jewish Law "Halakhah" (https://www.okclarity.com>glossary>Halakhah)

Acts 15:5
Acts 15:10-11 NLT
Acts 15:19 NLT
Acts 15:28-29
Acts 15:31
Romans 6:14

CHAPTER FOUR

First Pentecost:
Jewish Tradition has it that the first Pentecost coincided with the day God gave the Ten Commandments. (https://wwwligenier.org>Learn>Devotions)

2 Corinthians 3:6 NIV
John 19:30

"It is finished" Greek word "Tetelestai" Matthew 27:50-51
"Tetelestai", which means, "paid in full." This was the cry of a winner, because Jesus fully paid the debt of sin we owed, and finished the eternal purpose of the cross.
(Enduring Word Commentary, enduringword.com)

Exodus 30:10
Hebrews 8:10,12 NLT
Acts 13:38-39

Cartoon of "Dennis the Menace"

"Euangelion" Greek for "good news"
(*Expository Dictionary of New Testament Words* W.E. Vine)

Isaiah 59:2
Psalm 66:18

CHAPTER FIVE

Romans 8:39
Jeremiah 17:9
Romans 6:17
2 Chronicles 7:14
Luke 5:37-38

Hebrew word "Babel" means "confusion by mixing or a confused mixture" (en.wiktionary.org)

Genesis 11:7-8
Colossians 1:22 NLT

CHAPTER SIX

Sir Robert Robert Watson, the Scotsman who invented radar. (Microwaves101.com)

2 Corinthians 10:3-5 TPT
John 8:31-32 TPT

Hebrews 4:16
2 Corinthians 5:21
Hebrews 10:11-12
Hebrews 10:14
Hebrews 10:10
1 John 1:9
1 John 1:1-2
1 John 1:3
1 John 1:8,10
1 John 2:1
1 Corinthians 6:19-20
1 John 1:7

CHAPTER SEVEN

Hebrews 9:15
Hebrews 9:17
Hebrews 10:19-22 NIV
Hebrews 8:13
Matthew 23:2-3a NIV
Matthew 7:1 NIV
Matthew 5:22 NIV
Mark 10:19
Matthew 5:27
Matthew 6:14-15
Ephesians 4:32
Luke 24:46-47
John 14:6
Luke 24:17-19
Luke 24:26

CHAPTER EIGHT

Rare Chinese Bowl found at Garage sale - sells for 2.25 million. (https://wallstreetinsanity.com>rare-chinese -bowl-found)

John 16:7-11
Acts 1:4-5
Acts 1:8

Greek word "dunamis" which means "miracle working power " #1411 *The New Strongs Exhaustive Concordance of Bible*. James Strong, LL.D., S.T.D.

Alfred Nobel created gunpowder (en.wikipdia.org)

Acts 2:1-4

Hebrew word "ruach" refers to God as "a breath, a wind, or a life force that sustains all living things, human beings being included."

Acts 2:8

Language "dialektos"

Acts 2:8
"And how is it that we hear, each in our own language in which we were born? Parthians and Medes and Elamites, those dwelling in Mesopotamia, Judea and Cappadocia, Pontus and Asia, Phrygia and Pamphylia, Egypt and the parts of Libya adjoining Cyrene, visitors from Rome, both Jews and proselytes, Cretans and Arabs—we hear them speaking in our own tongues the wonderful works of God."

These were not general languages but according to the Greek word "dialekto" which is where we get our word dialect this particular form of a language is peculiar to a specific region or social group.

Acts 5:5-8
1 Corinthians 6:19
1 Peter 2:9
Romans 12:1

CHAPTER NINE

How To Live Like A King's Kid: The Miracle Way of Living That Has Changed Millions of Lives
By Harold Hill (author) Irene Harrell

Acts 16:9-10
Proverbs 29:25 b

CHAPTER TEN

Greek word "ecclesia" - unusual because it was not a religious word. It meant "gathering of those summoned," in ancient Greece, "assembly of citizens in a city-state." (https://www.britannica.com>topic>Ecclesia-ancient-Greek-assembly)

Matthew 28:18-20
Luke 24:49
Acts 2:16-18
Acts 2:36-39

Albert Einstein's statement:
Albert Einstein said, "There are only two ways to live your life. One is as though nothing is a miracle. The other is as though everything is." (https://brainquote.com>com>authors>Albert-Einstein)

Planet facts

Speeding through space at 67,000 miles an hour (https://www.space.com)

23,000 breaths a day (https://www.bbc.com>work life>article)

Average heart will beat 100,000 times today circulating 5 quarts of blood through 60,000 miles of arteries, veins, and capillaries. (livescience.com, Circulatory system)

Isaiah 53:5
1 Peter 2:24
Mark 6:5-6
John 20:21-22
Acts 10:45-46
1 Corinthians 14:18
Matthew 24:11
2 Timothy 1:7
Acts 10:38
James 4:7
John 14:12
Romans 1:16a
Romans 15:17-19

CHAPTER ELEVEN

1 Thessalonians 5:23
John 3:6
James 1:23-25

When you look in a mirror, you're not actually seeing your face, you are seeing a reflection of your face. You have never really seen your face, but you can trust the image in your mirror to reflect back to you what you look like.

Andrew Wommack 2008 *Spirit, Soul, and Body* Harrison House
Publishers pg.2-4, Tulsa, OK 74153 (www.harrisonhouse.com)

Genesis 2:16-17
Romans 5:12
Romans 5:17
2 Corinthians 5:21 NIV
Ephesians 2:1
Colossians 1:21-22
Ephesians 1:13-14

When someone cans food, they seal the jars with paraffin, which
makes an airtight seal that will protect and preserve the food within.
This is how the word "seal" is used in this verse. When you were
born again, your spirit was immediately vacuum packed by the Holy
Spirit, keeping the good in and the bad out.

Spirt Soul and Body, Andrew Wommack, copyright 2005,
published by Harrison House Publishers, Tulsa, Ok 74153 (www.
harrisonhouse.com)

Ephesians 4:24b
John 4:17
2 Corinthians 6:7
1 John 2:20
1 Corinthians 2:16
1 Corinthians 3:1-3

In the Greek, the word "carnal" is "sarkikos," meaning being led
by the flesh; of the senses; being led by an unrenewed mind; being
governed by human nature, instead of by the Spirit of God.

An Expository Dictionary of New Testament Words, W. E. Vine,
M.A., Fleming H. Revel Company, Old Tappa, New Jersey,
Seventeenth impression 1966

Philemon 1:6

The word "effective" is the Greek word "energeo." It denotes active, powerful in action where we get our English word "energy." *Vines Expository Dictionary of Old and New Testament Words*, W.E. Vine, Old Testament Edited By F.F. Bruce, Fleming H. Revell Company, Old Tappan, New Jersey

2 Peter 1:3-4

CHAPTER TWELVE

Arthur Barry, a Newell thief, Worlds ul-timate.net

Stats on Identity theft
(https://www.definefinancial.com>Blog)

Genesis 3:6
2 Corinthians 5:21
Our amazing DNA
(https://wwwin.kqed.org<alongwindingDNA)

Dr. Caroline Leaf, author of the book *Switch On Your Brain*
(https://www.goodreads.com>773964.caroline_leaf)

A DOWNLOAD FOR AN UPLIFT

9 phrases to help you stay up in a down world:

"Faith, not fear; positive, not negative; hope, not despair; courage, not discouraged; strength, not weakness; built up, not torn down; fearless, not fretful; prayerful, not anxious; bold, not timid." -Mike Rose

1 John 4:4
Colossians 2:9-10
Hebrews 1:2